FEMININE JURISPRUDENCE IN INDIA

Women's Right

FEMININE JURISPRUDENCE IN INDIA

Women's Right

Edited by
DR. GOKULESH SHARMA
Judge, Civil Court, Lucknow

DEEP & DEEP PUBLICATIONS PVT. LTD.
F-159, Rajouri Garden, New Delhi-110027

FEMININE JURISPRUDENCE IN INDIA
WOMEN'S RIGHT

ISBN 978-81-8450-037-0

Typeset by ASHISH TECHNOGRAPHICS,
3190, Mohindra Park, Shakur Basti, Delhi-110034.

Printed in India at NEW ELEGANT PRINTERS,
A-49/1, Maya Puri, Phase-I, New Delhi-110064.

Published by DEEP & DEEP PUBLICATIONS PVT. LTD.
F-159, Rajouri Garden, New Delhi-110027.
Phones: 25435369, 25440916
E-mail: ddpbooks@yahoo.co.in • deep98@del3.vsnl.net.in
Showroom:
2/13, Ansari Road, Daryaganj, New Delhi-110002 • Telefax: 23245122

Contents

Preface

The worldly affairs are not complete without woman. No one can come into existence without mother. Motherhood is a essential aspect of society and always respected and remembered in every walk of life, in every pact of society, in jungle, even in animals and birds, motherhood is a predominant factor which can not be ignored.

It is a disappointing feature of our society that motherhood and womanhood is not respected in due sense, rather it is ignored. The priority of man against woman and dominance of masculine against feminism is a progressive factor. Since time immemorial womanhood is subject to several kinds of cruelties, inhuman behaviour and treatment. In substance it can be said that womanhood is treated as the property of man only. Inferiority of women is an admitted factor since long time. Even this weaker sex could not raise voice against it or that voice was crushed by men for his own benefit or dominance over women. No religious community or sector or nation has exception to this practice of suppression of woman by the male community at large.

Without commenting upon any nation, how so ever progressive or advanced these may be, their feeling toward woman is not proper. They think woman only inferior to them and subject to their rule.

Our nation India, in ancient time was exception to it. The man and woman were treated as par. Kings and Queens always went to battlefield along with soldiers. The respect of ladies and women was very high. They were regarded as "Laxmi" (Graha Laxmi). Even in some part, these women enjoyed more and more privileges and rights. They were in comfortable status. The status of ladies in ancient India was as with men. The education of ladies were at peak. Woman were also looking kingdom and discharged administrative function. In substance it may be concluded that ladies and women enjoyed equal status with man in ancient India along with few other privileges.

The position in near past and medieval period deteriorated continuously. and slowly. Various factors were responsible for it. The main factor was the invasion of foreigners over India and imposition of their culture and system over us. Then cosmopolitan culture started. We lost our own culture and its purity. Confusion of culture and invasion of foreigners consequently exploitation of foreign rule resulted in the down-gradation of women and their status. They slowly lost their status, equality and lastly they became without any kind of status. They further lost the privileges they enjoyed earlier. They became the property of man and accordingly they were dealt. It lasted up 1947, the independence of nation raised a ray of hope to these women who were without status. Slowly and gradually privileges have been granted to them. An attempt has been made to treat them equally with man. Equality is offered to them in all respect. Still we have to travel a long journey. We have not granted any thing special. They have been provided with those rights which are supposed to be their own and these were snatched from them earlier. We have to fit in society equally we have to remain equally in all walk of life, then only the equality of man and woman can be achieved in true sense. We have continuously to work hard in this direction in future so that the present gap and discrimination of status may vanish in future.

I have tried to bring in the present book, the plights of woman. Plights and worries of woman from the mouth of women can be better understood. I have compiled few best essays and published papers of eminent woman jurist who are devoted to the causes of woman. It is called feminist jurisprudence. Their feeling is thought, their working is theory, their action is concept. Still the feminist jurisprudence is at childhood. They are trying to outrage the problems of woman. They are not working against any man or society. There is a apprehension in the mind of gentlemen of society that these are working against us is a false fear. They are trying to show their problems. They want to come to a status of equality with man only. Hence we should see the feminist jurisprudence with special care. Necessary assistance should also be provided to them. No hurdle should be created rather we should also try to remove hurdles.

We cannot put assistance to woman, when we are coming across to their problems and worries. They may put their plight and problem through published paper, writing, media or otherwise. We can know these problems. I have attempted to collect these problems, plight and worries of woman from their own voice in their own language. I have compiled work of writers in this regard. I think I have put roughly the problem of woman which they are facing at present for their redressal. I have counted problems of woman in society. It is now our turn for the solution of these problems.

The book has been written with special reference to woman in India. Relevant instances of foreign countries have also been adopted.

The book has been divided in six chapters. First chapter deals with Introduction, i.e. problem of woman. Second chapter deals with the philosophy why man is reasonable why not woman in legal sense. Third chapter describes feminist approaches of human rights, i.e. special human right of ladies. Fourth chapter in with regard to legal education of woman in India. Fifth chapter is a detailed study of comparative human right of woman and man. Sixth and final chapter is a conclusion what should be done in India in future for woman.

I have also kept in view the volume of book so that it may not be so voluminous that the reader may not feel it to read or to carry. All essays have been dealt with due care in the language of imminent writer. If any mistake is discovered or if any omission or otherwise problem is brought to my knowledge, then I tend all due apologies in advance for the same and consequently I call for suggestion from the readers of the book for correction in future.

The book is dedicated to my elder brother Late Pandit Sunder Lal Sharma Ji, whole high inspiration and blessings persuaded me to studies for the welfare of society at large with special attention to woman because he thought it as a tribute to motherhood.

The credit of this goes to my better half Smt. Neela Sharma who has not only helped me, but also advised me about the problem of woman. I have special regard to my children Sanju, Sakshi, Kriti and Vasistha. They have also cooperated me to write the book. Finally, I am grateful to publisher Deep & Deep Publications Pvt. Ltd., New Delhi through Shree G.S. Bhatia who has published the book in time.

I hope that the book shall be highly useful for ladies and women and to all concerned who have special regard to all either to motherhood or womanhood.

DR. GOKHULESH SHARMA
Judge, Lucknow

1

Introduction Gender Problem in Law

ARCHANA PARASHAR AND AMITA DHANDA

In consonance with the title of the book, this introduction has been divided into two parts. The first part has been written by Archana Parashar and the second by Amita Dhanda.

I. ENGENDERING LAW

The Indian feminist movement started off with an optimistic reliance on the power of the law to deliver social reform and is now in danger of rejecting any meaningful engagement with the law. In either case there is an unnecessarily narrow conception of the nature of law. What exactly is meant by the concept of nature of law is more or less the question at the centre of this book. There is no one universally accepted answer to this question but it is important to consider whether any one conception is better than another. A failure to justify any particular conception of law leads to relativism and the consequential situation where it is not possible to pursue any common goals. I wish to argue that a feminist understanding of law is essential for anyone interested in achieving social justice through the law and I would like to believe that no one can absolve themselves of the responsibility to pursue social justice for all members of society.

The central premise of the book is assumed rather than argued for, that law is an important institution of the contemporary Indian society. Therefore, feminists' response to law must be an informed response rather than based on incomplete or inadequate understanding of the nature of law and its relationships with other institutions of society like the polity, economy or civil society. This is where the legal feminists have a special role to play-to provide the kinds of legal analyses unfortunately missing from much of Indian scholarship on law. There is a healthy diversity of views amongst feminists and the same should be expected to be true of legal feminists. It is, therefore, suggested that legal feminists united in their pursuit of gender justice but what constitutes gender justice may be defined various analysts.

Legal feminists by their very nature operate in the wider context of legal scholarship than that which focuses primarily on legal positivism. The first task for legal feminists therefore is to challenge the pervasive hold of legal positivism in the field of legal analyses and, secondly, to argue for the relevance of gender in any analysis of law. This argument has two broad parts: that legal analyses should encompass a broader theoretical base than the normative legal theory of jurisprudence and that legal scholarship must be socially responsible. And an obvious way of achieving that is by making gender a central concern of legal theory. In the following sections I will elaborate these two issues separately.

Why Theory

Within the academic discipline of law, it is still an unresolved issue whether the study of law belongs in the universities or it is a professional training best imparted by its practitioners. Even though law is now taught in universities everywhere, in legal scholarship the dichotomy between doctrinal study of law and a wider understanding of law as one among many institutions of society has continued to persist. Thus, theory of law can either mean normative theory of law dealing with legal doctrine, the conventional understanding of jurisprudence, or it can encompass inter-disciplinary understandings of law including sociological, historical, anthropological, etc. analyses. I wish to argue for the latter understanding of the theoretical study of law but before that a brief explanation of the contemporary state of legal scholarship in India is necessary.

India as a post-colonial State operates with a common law system of law. The current state of legal scholarship is partly a reflection of the hold of legal positivist ideas that were dominant when the British law tradition was transferred to India. Even though India is now an independent State, it continues to be a common law system and there is no realistic move or option to jettison the imported legal tradition. It is also a curious but probably inevitable effect of an imposed system of law that while the colonizing nation and its laws continue to adapt in response to their transformed needs the imposed or transferred institutions in the former colonies become ever more anachronistic. The ideas about law in India are neither a straightforward application of contemporary ideas in Britain nor other common law jurisdictions like the USA nor are the Indian law scholars free to abandon the constraints of common law principles (and procedures).

This assertion can be illustrated with the help of two random examples. In Indian law we still apply the doctrine of dependent domicile of the wife while the contemporary British law has abandoned this concept. Similarly, Indian lawyers continue to apply the concept of restitution of conjugal rights, while the concept no longer exists in the English legal system. In both cases Indian women suffer the brunt of anachronistic rules with virtually no accountability of the legal system. Even if there was some justification initially for imposing these doctrines on Indian society there is no valid reason for continuing with them in the present day context. Sure, the law as introduced in the 1800s has not remained static, both statutory and judicial developments have happened ever since but in many ways there is no systematic rationale for these changes. And very often the weight of inertia is much greater than any effort at change.

The reason for making this somewhat obvious point is that the kind of legal scholarship considered appropriate is similarly affected by the past. The state of contemporary Indian legal scholarship shows an overwhelming reliance on positivist ideas about the law. I recognize that there are notable exceptions to this sweeping generalization and also wish to emphasize that this argument is not about personal failures of legal scholars or about their reading and writing habits. My argument is that institutionally the conception of legal knowledge is primarily a positivist conception. This exclusive concern with legal doctrine is not a considered choice of a perspective on law but more likely a continuation of the colonial ideas of legal positivism.

Historically the introduction of common law into India happened in a piecemeal fashion but it is widely accepted that the British positivists could experiment with their new ideas about law in India in a way not possible in England. Thus, the legal codes we still live by like the Indian Penal Code, the Criminal Procedure Code and the Contract Act are enduring legacies of that era and world-view. The rise of legal positivism is variously explained and this is not the place to discuss these theories but one theory is that the view of law as the command of the sovereign was necessitated by the rise of the modern State. The significance of this explanation lies in that it sought to displace the hold of earlier common law idea that law is binding because it is the expression of immemorial custom of the people. It is easy to see why the change in the political system and the creation of the modern State also gave rise to a new conception of the authority and nature of law. The classical common law understanding that judges and not the legislators were the knowers of law and technically the legislators did not create new laws was not particularly well suited to imperial expansion. The classical positivist understanding of law as the command of the sovereign was more suitable for the colonizing enterprise and was relied upon by the British administrators in India.

For most of the last century legal theory in common law has sought to answer the fundamental question of why law is authoritatively binding and invariably the background context for this analysis is the claim of common law as representing the accumulated wisdom of a community.[1] However, legal scholarship in India by and large does not concern itself with justifying the authority of the law and therefore, mechanistic analyses of the doctrine seem like sufficient analyses. The resultant paucity of legal theory suitable for the specific contexts of Indian women thus is not surprising.

Legal theory and the legal profession have always existed with a certain amount of tension in the common law tradition. It is true that the relevance of jurisprudence for the practice of law has never been unequivocally accepted. But I argue that even practitioners need to understand the nature of the doctrine they work with, why is it in any particular form, could it be different and how interpretation plays a role in attributing meaning to the content of doctrine. In order to be able to do so the kind of legal theory one uses becomes important. But before arguing for a particular kind of legal theory I will briefly discuss the somewhat tenuous hold of theory in legal scholarship.

The common law conception of law as accumulated wisdom of community does not give the philosophers of laws an exalted position. However, for a long time jurisprudence or what Cotterrell calls normative theory of law has coexisted with the conception of law as specialized technical knowledge. According to Cotterrell[2] the transformations in law necessitated a shift in lawyers' understanding of law. The emphasis in classical common law on the content or substance of legal doctrine was replaced with the emphasis on the form of law, that is, something was law if it was properly enacted by the appropriate authority.

I accept Cotterrell's explanation that the concerns of normative legal theory are partly a reflection of the efforts of legal philosophers to impose a system and structure in legal

---

1. I will not go into the details or discussion of various theories of the nature of law. For an introduction see Roger Cotterrell, 'The Politics of Jurisprudence: A Critical Introduction to Legal Philosophy', Butterworths, London, 1989.
2. Roger Cotterrell, 'The Uses of Theory', *Id.* at pp. 216-35.

ideas. However, normative theory is not only an effort to gain academic prestige for a profession. It is also an effort to examine seriously how law can gain integrity as the means by which human beings impose reason, to the limits of their ability, on the otherwise chaotic conditions of their social existence."[3] The claims of jurisprudence become mystificatory only when it ignores its obvious partial perspective and claims to be explaining in some a historical, timeless sense, the nature of law.

The exclusive emphasis of normative theory on legal doctrine came to be challenged in turn by legal realists, the law and society movement, then by critical legal theorists and more recently by feminist and minority scholars.[4] The resultant empirical legal theory analyses the social, economic and political context of legal doctrine. This focus enables an understanding of law as an institution of society inter-linked with all other institutions. Empirical legal theory can therefore better explain legal change and the links between social and legal changes.

Nonetheless this empirical shift in legal theory is not entirely at the cost of normative legal theory or jurisprudence or legal philosophy which still occupies centre stage in much of legal scholarship. As yet it is unusual to find legal education designed as free from the paradigm imposed by normative legal theory. The empirical legal theory insights are accepted on the margins but have not displaced the dominance of conventional doctrine as the subject-matter of legal knowledge. I believe that it is important to accept the point made by Cotterrell that the problem with normative legal theory (or any theory) is in its failure to accept its partial perspective. For legal theory to be truly inclusive it must acknowledge the partial perspective of normative legal ideas. I wish to argue that feminist critiques of legal theory explicate this partial perspective most effectively and therefore, it is important that everyone takes feminist insights about the nature of legal (and any other) knowledge into account.

---

3. *Id.* at p. 229.
4. For a good account of these developments, see R. Cotterrell, 'Sociology of Laws: An Introduction', Butterworths, London (2nd edn.), 1992, and *supra* n. 1 at pp. 231-35.

Legal Theory in India

Most of these relatively recent developments in broader legal theory do not find a systematic place in Indian legal writings. The reason for this I suggest is that, as argued above, the conception of common law as the accumulated wisdom of a community never really took hold on the Indian subcontinent. Consequently the introduction of legal positivist ideas was not and has not been challenged ever since. As a consequence legal writing is mostly confined to the analysis of legal doctrine, i.e. examining the details of judgments and legislation. There is no means of explaining why the law has binding authority, why does the law have this particular shape or form, or whether law can be expected to help in achieving social change or what can be done when law is actually hindering social transformation. That is, no theoretical explanations are available other than relatively mechanistic applications of normative theory. The significance of empirical legal theories is not obvious as neither the lawyers nor the majority of legal academics consider these developments to be relevant to them.

The immediate issue therefore, is whether these relatively recent western developments in legal theory have any relevance for Indian legal scholars and feminists. In the context of post-colonial Indian society the hostility to western ideas is understandable and it is no surprise then that most Indian lawyers can claim that they choose not to pursue ideas about law as they develop in western scholarship. This attitude is understandable but not necessarily conducive to generating a critical legal analysis tradition. More importantly it tries to overlook the obvious reality that the legal system operating in India is not an indigenous institution. Since no one is seriously contemplating replacing this system and it regulates almost all aspects of our lives, it is imperative that a systematic analysis of the legal system is undertaken. Legal scholars are in the best position to discharge this responsibility as unlike judges and practising lawyers they have the necessary distance and independence from legal institutions to be able to critique them. Their institutional situation and expertise also equip them to engage in theoretical critique of the law. I would now like to explain what could be an appropriate theoretical analysis.

As indicated above I consider normative legal theory to be a partial perspective. It is important to understand that this is not a particular failing of normative legal theory but that any theoretical perspective can only ever be partial. However, this need not be an argument for not theorizing. Even though Cotterrell[5] makes a distinction between normative and empirical legal theory, he argues that it should be possible to bridge the gap between these two very broad perspectives. Empirical legal theory treats law as a social phenomenon, which must be examined through systematic empirical analyses of the political, economic and social conditions in which it exists. It enables an examination of legal change in a systematic fashion as it focuses on political, economic and social contexts of the legal doctrine. This is the kind of legal theory necessary for understanding the role of law in contemporary Indian society. It is obvious that such theory can only be inter-disciplinary and I suggest that feminist scholarship offers the conceptual tools necessary to develop specifically Indian legal theory.

I would also like to emphasize that the division between theory and practice is something I find problematic. This division finds expression in legal as well as feminist writings and very often is a critique of the impracticality or abstractness of theory. Arguably every action is based on certain assumptions. Whether those assumptions are justifiable or not, and if yes, by reference to what, are the basic questions everyone—lawyer or feminist, theorist or activist, must answer. Theory compels us to articulate and justify our assumptions. In the process it also enables us to identify assumptions made in others' views and thus critique them.[6]

---

5. *Supra* n. 1 at pp. 231-35.
6. See Bell Hooks, "Theory as Liberatory Practice", 4, *Yale Journal of Law and Feminism*, 1991, p. 7: Sneja Gunew, Feminist Knowledge: Critique and Construct", in S. Gunew (ed.), Feminist Knowledge: Critique and Construct", Routledge, London, 1990, pp. 3-44.

The single most significant contribution of academic feminism is that it has made gender a relevant category in all disciplines. Prior to the rise of feminist ideas the prevalent norms of theorizing portrayed knowledge as neutral and universal. Law was no exception to this trend and to an extent is still resistant to the demands for change. It is only with the help of gender as a category of analysis that the claims of universality and neutrality of knowledge can be challenged. The relevance of gender cannot be argued for unless the basic assumptions of the universal and neutral theories are analyzed. The concept of gender is itself a contested concept.[7] Thus, a feminist theoretical perspective makes explicit the unstated assumptions of much of the conventional legal theory. For example, feminists have shown that what counts as a neutral standard in law is invariably the male norm. Only it is classified as a neutral norm with the result that men can conform to the norm without difficulty while women are constantly left struggling.[8] I suggest that gender must become a fundamental category of legal analysis not only for feminists but all legal scholars.

Feminists Engagements with Law

The history of western feminist engagement with law is conventionally traced to the demand for equal legal rights by suffragists. Women demanded and eventually gained civil rights. An increasing parity of rights between men and women led to the realization that mere sameness between men and women in the public sphere was not enough to change the socially subordinate position of women. Some feminists thus argued that non-oppression or non-discrimination for women involved recognition of the differences between men and women. While others insisted that men and women should be treated the same. These two standpoints manifested as the famous sameness/difference

7. See for example, Anne Edwards, 'The Sex/Gender Distinction: Has it outlived its Usefulness?', 10 Australian Feminist Studies, 1989, pp. 1-12 and other articles in this issue of the Australian Feminist Studies.
8. Ngaire Naffine, Law and the Sexes: Explorations in Feminist Jurisprudence, Allen and Unwin, Sydney, 1990.

debates in feminist and legal feminist writings. The central issue here became the definition of equality: whether legal equality meant same treatment and formal equality or could it accommodate differences and ensure substantive equality. In feminist legal literature the central issue in the equality debates was regarding the relevance of gender differences for law. That is, whether laws ought to be gender-neutral or gender-specific. There was of course the question whether gender differences could be identified unproblematically or the issue was what specific characteristics constitute gender. Further obvious problems lay in deciding whether the empirical differences were biological and immutable or socially constructed and thus changeable. Discussions of these and similar issues, i.e. whether it could be ascertained with any certainty what constitutes a woman, came to be classified as the essentialism debates.

There are two broad aspects of the essentialism argument, one argument is raised by 'ethnic' women (thereby meaning non-Anglo women in first world countries). That gender is not the only relevant difference and feminism must take into account differences of race, national origin, religion, sexuality, class *et al.* A slightly different argument is raised by post-structuralists that just like any other term the category cannot be given a fixed, final and undisputed meaning. From both these standpoints it can follow thereby that it is virtually impossible to make any overarching claims in the name of women or feminism. And thus it has been suggested that post-structuralism makes it problematic to have any feminist politics but I will return to this issue later.[9]

This is a very brief thumb-nail sketch of the developments in feminist thought and the purpose of providing this chronology is to argue that for every stage of feminist critique there is a corresponding feminist legal view

9. For a brief introduction to these developments see Alison Jagger, Feminist Politics and Human Nature, Rowman and Liulefield Publishers Inc., New Jersey, 1983; Linda Nicholson (ed.), Feminism/ Postmodernisms, Routledge, New York, 1990; Elizabeth Spelman, Inessential Woman: Problems of Exclusion in Feminist Thought, Beacon Press, Boston, 1988.

with a specific conception of the law.[10] So, the first feminist efforts in the suffragist movement to gain equal legal rights for women were based upon the standard Liberal legal paradigm. The normative understanding of the law was that it is about neutral, universal principles. Early feminists accepted this view and they simply sought to extend it to women. Since the Liberal legal feminists did not question the claims of neutrality and universality of legal norms they could only argue for gender neutrality of the laws. The early feminists used the Liberal arguments to show the irrationality of treating women less favourably than men and could thus demand for women the same legal rights as men.[11]

Formal legal equality for women was one of the earlier gains of the feminist movement. However, formal legal equality did not result in eradication of women's subordination. Some feminist theorists therefore began to critique the assumptions on which Liberal thought is constructed and were able to explain how sexuality constitutes the basis of different positions of men and women. In Liberal paradigm sexuality is a private sphere issue and thus not relevant to the public or political sphere. The feminists' focus on the artificiality of the public/private division has resulted in questioning the naturalness of the sexual division of labour.[12]

---

10. Without trying to give an exhaustive bibliography the following books are suggested as a suitable starting-point for entering the literature on feminist legal scholarship: Cynthia Fuchs Epstein, Women in Law, Anchor Books, Doubleday, New York, USA, 1981; Rosemarie Tong, Women, Sex and the Law, Rowe and Allanheld, New Jersey, USA, 1984; Frances Olsen (ed.), Feminist Legal Theory, Aldershot, Hants, Dartmouth, 1994.
11. See for example, Mary Wollstonecraft, Vindication of the Rights of Woman, Penguin Books, Harmondsworth, 1982; Elizabeth Kingdom, 'Gendering Rights', in A.J. Arnaud and E. Kingdom (eds.), Women's Rights amid the Rights of Men, Aberdeen University Press, Glasgow, 1990.
12. There is vast feminist literature on the public/private divide. As a start see Genevive Lloyd, Time Man of Reason: 'Male' and 'Female' in Western Philosophy, Metheun, London, 1984, Margaret Thornton (ed.), Public and Private: Feminist Legal Debates, Oxford University Press, Melbourne, 1996.

The interdependence of the public and private spheres makes a mockery of the idea that law only regulates the public sphere. The kind of legal reform that follows from this analysis thus necessarily challenges the formal equality model as well as the notion that the private sphere is the sphere of freedom from legal regulation. For example, the issue of what constitutes justice in family law necessarily must use an understanding of law as inter-linked to the prevailing sexual division of labour. If at the end of a marriage formal rules of private property are applied most women will be left without any assets and/or income. In the strict doctrinal interpretation and application of rules of property law there is nothing wrong with the outcome that property goes to the one who has legal ownership. However, this is not the only interpretation available. Feminists have shown that a 'just' family law must recognize that most married women perform unpaid work.

Feminist analyses explain how the man is able to accumulate property or gain the income-generating capacity only because he has a wife looking after the day-to-day concerns of himself and his family. The neat division between public and private spheres overlooks the fact that the public sphere activities undertaken by men are only possible because there is a particular kind of private sphere inhabited by women.[13] That is, the ideal worker is a man who can perform all his duties because he lives with a wife. The family law should recognize this social reality and, therefore, at the end of a marriage the law must recognize the right of the wife to a share in the matrimonial property. Conventional property rules that accept the legal title as the final proof of ownership or entitlement serve the interests of men but not of most women. This analysis conceptualizes law as operating in a specific social and economic context and it brings into the argument the effects of gender hierarchy. It necessarily moves beyond the narrow conception of law as the extant doctrine and questions the effects of legal concepts like the public and private division.

---

13. Ross Poole, Morality and Modernity, Routledge, London, New York, 1991.

The question however, is whether it is incumbent upon everyone to accept this feminist perspective. For example, if someone claims not to be a feminist should they have to accept a feminist analysis? What about the women who choose to be full time mothers and wives and do not wish to demean their actions by putting an economic value on them? I will discuss the latter question first.

Radical feminists have made it possible to examine the construction of masculinity and femininity in social and political discourses. The fundamental assumption here is that women's subordination will not end as long as issues of sexuality are not addressed. As a consequence it is the construction of femininity that takes prominence in radical feminist discourse. This focus of analysis has shifted right out of the Liberal paradigm and displaced the prominence of the so-called political sphere.[14] The idea that femininity is a social construct challenges the argument that women and men have different, identifiable characteristics. But it goes further and explains how it is not a matter of choice for women (and men) to transcend the constraints of femininity (or masculinity).[15] Thus, the fact that most women choose to be primary parents at the cost of self-advancement or financial independence is not adequately explainable as a function of individual choice. Rather, it shows how individual choices are constructed by the prevailing ideologies.

The corresponding legal feminist views thus focus not on suitable law reform as in the statutory law of rape or domestic violence but on the wider processes of trial and the experiences of the women complainants. The reform process of law must go beyond the demand for a change of technical rules and demand a transformation of the conventional understanding of law. Instead of restricting our understanding of law to the technicalities of the rules it

14. Ziliah Eisenstein, 'Time Female Body and Time Lou', University of California Press, Berkeley, California, 1988.
15. Sandra Lee Berkeley, 'Foucault, Femininity, and The Modernisation of Patriarchal Power', in Irene Diamond and Lee Quinby (eds.), Feminism and Foucault, North Eastern University Press, Boston, 1988, pp. 61-83.

requires a focus on the processes of construction of the meaning of law. Legal conventions that construct a rape victim as liable to tell untruth or the accuser as in need of protection are social constructs and there is nothing inevitable about not trusting a rape. victim's story. Why does the law adopt these constructs therefore becomes the subject of feminist analysis. It at once challenges the neutrality of legal rules and demonstrates the partial nature of legal assumptions. It also shows the connections between legal assumptions and social constructs of femininity. It follows that the legal theorists must move beyond analyzing the details of legal doctrine and concern themselves with how legal knowledge is formed.

Such an understanding of law at once demonstrates the connections between the law and other societal institutions. At the very least the law's claim of autonomy no longer seems plausible. It is not surprising that the connection between social and legal constructs sometimes leads to a defeatist attitude that what is required is wider social change and mere changes in the law will not change the position of women as law is a limited instrument. One version of the 'limits of law' argument is that law is a crude instrument, not particularly well suited to bringing about social transformation. Early Marxist analyses exhibit this attitude.[16] A more recent version of the argument relies on Foucault's analysis to say that by focussing on law feminists have given undue importance to law and that the law ought to be decentered.[17] This line of analysis is also described, as the post-modernist development in legal scholarship and a persistent trend in post-modern analyses of law is to debunk the idea that law can yield desirable social change.

Post-modern thought is difficult to define but at the very least it has challenged the conventional view of objective knowledge. At the risk of sounding simplistic I suggest that

16. See for example articles in, B. Fine, R. Kinsey, J. Lea, S. Picciotto and J. Young (eds.), Capitalism and The Rule of Law: From Deviancy Theory to Marxism, Hutchinson, London, 1979.

17. Carol Smart is the most well-known proponent of this view. See Carol Smart, Feminism and the Power of Law, London, 1989.

post-modernism is about the foundations of knowledge and therefore it is of direct relevance to the study of law.[18] As Margaret Davies argues. The post-modern, while not dispensing with legitimation, challenges pre-existing methods of legitimation, and in particular, at the present time, the idea of universal, abstract principles of legitimation. The post-modern condition therefore describes an intellectual challenge to the assumptions and foundations of western thought."[19] In legal analyses a post-modern perspective brings into focus issues otherwise obscured from view. For example, the claim that law consists of universal and abstract principles provides legitimation to the legal system. But once it is asked how the laws are experienced by the differently situated persons, what values are incorporated in the laws and how they affect different sections of community, or how the same individual experiences different aspects of the legal system it becomes obvious that law operates at many levels and differently for different people. It is not plausible to talk about law as a single entity. However, does it also mean that there is no such thing as law and therefore I can not analyze it or anything goes? I do not think so.

Post-structural thought carries forward the critique of objective knowledge by challenging the distinction between the subject and the discrete system, which is the object of theory. Post-structuralists argue that the existence of a self-contained or autonomous subject is as improbable as of a similarly self-contained system. Thus, the knower and the known are mutually constituted. Not that there is no already existing reality waiting to be discovered, there is no possibility of an objective subject/observer/knower who is untouched or unaffected by what he or she is observing. This standpoint has enormous significance for understanding the nature of law. Thus, the law's insistence on its nature being specialized knowledge which has a definite meaning can be deconstructed show how the insistence on such a view

---

18. The following section draws upon Margaret Davies, Asking The Law Question, The Law Book Company, Sydney, pp. 224-54.
19. *Id.* at p. 227.

excludes those who do not share the dominant view. That the meaning of law can be authoritatively determined is an equal fallacy. It simply allows for one interpretation to gain dominance at the cost of another. Thus, post-structuralism allows for diversity of meanings to exist.

So too the assertion that law is simply the law of the sovereign State misses the point that the law gets its meaning from the intersection of legal and various other social systems of meaning. Social conventions interact with legal norms in many different ways—sometimes to enforce and at other times to delegitimize the institutionalized norms. The task of legal analysts therefore must be to unravel how various levels of meanings are constituted institutionally. The single most important point for any legal theory therefore is the acceptance of the idea that meaning—including legal meaning—is constructed rather than pre-existing and simply waiting to be discovered.

I wish to argue that law like any other institution of society is interconnected with other institutions. It is futile to expect law to deliver a revolution but at the same time it is not possible to disengage from the law. The task of legal scholars therefore, is to explicate the connections between the law and social, political, and economic systems. If a particular kind of economy and a specific form of law are coexistent it does not help for legal theory to ignore the connections. But at the same time law scholars must guard against a mechanistic application of theories from other disciplines. The interdisciplinary study of law by lawyers must mean that they bring their knowledge of the doctrine and analyze it in the context of the knowledge of other disciplines. In doing so they carry the responsibility to try and realize the highest aspirations of their profession, i.e. to achieve social justice for all. As Cotterrell says, "the task . . . is to explore sociologically the conditions under which law can become a principled component of social life, a direct expression of community interests, structures and concerns."[20]

---

20. Roger Cotterrell, "Socio-Legal Studies: Between Policy and Community" in his book, Law's Community, Clarendon Press, Oxford, 1995 at p. 301.

It is of course true that post-structuralists have made it very difficult if not impossible to say with confidence what is the meaning of terms like community interests or concerns. That is, if the meaning of any term can not be fixed absolutely does it follow that there is no way of judging that any interpretation should take precedence over others. This is the charge of relativism or indeterminacy against post-structuralism. I wish to argue that it is unnecessary to give such an interpretation to the implications of post-structural argument. It is important to remember that any interpretation happens in a context. Once the context is made explicit the purpose of any interpretation and the consequences flowing therefrom become relevant. Some feminists have argued that post-structural thought must be supplemented with the imperative that the resultant ideas or worldview do not become a legitimation for maintaining the *status quo* or to disadvantage any section of community. This is the only way in which law can accommodate diversity and at the same time pursue social justice.

It follows that it is not open to legal scholars, much less to feminist legal scholars to argue that their viewpoint is the only valid view. We as editors of this book have tried to live up to this expectation and represented many diverse conceptions of feminist legal analyses in this book. The writers come from various perspectives and work with different conceptions of the law. We hope that this introduction will be useful to the reader to contextualise each article. We have resisted the temptation to make every author conform to a particular conception of feminist analysis—even if that was possible it would not be desirable, as it would contravene our understanding that there is no single truth or reality. Which one of the different points of views does a reader wish to adopt remains for the individual to decide.

D.N. Saraf, Chandrasekharan Pillai, Ved Kumari, and S.P. Sathe have analysed the gender aspects of specific legislations or judgments. Although all these writers focus on gender issues they have emphasised different aspects of the relevance of gender.

D.N. Saraf has analysed aspects of the Consumer Protection Act, 1986 and argues that even though the Act is not gender specific it recognises a special place for women in relation to the redressal of consumer disputes. Saraf details the judicial developments in India with regard to medical negligence as very often women are affected parties in cases of pregnancy. He concludes that the concepts like informed consent must be interpreted in the specific social context of most Indians in lower economic strata. He also states that apart from financial constraints social factors prevent women from obtaining adequate services of medical professionals. Saraf suggests that the consumer protection law should use unconventional sources like the unfair trade practices principles rather than rely solely on the concepts of tort law. Saraf makes it obvious that judges make choices in interpreting legislation and B. Sivaramayya makes the same point with respect to legislative choices.

Chandrasekharan Pillai and Ved Kumari have discussed different aspects of criminal law. Ved Kumari has provided a close analysis of the legislative provisions of the Indian Penal Code. The Indian Penal Code is the main repository of criminal law and the assumptions on which it works have far-reaching consequences. Ved Kumari argues that these assumptions are based on an unproblematic acceptance of the public/private division and patriarchal values. She gives a detailed analysis of the specific provisions of the Indian Penal Code dealing with sexuality, rape and sexual assault and marriage-related crimes, i.e. adultery.

Ved Kumari has persuasively argued for the criminal law provisions to be gender sensitive and in the process demonstrated how the social and cultural context is important in giving meaning to legal provisions. Gender neutral laws can work to the advantage or disadvantage of women depending on the context. For example, criminal law holds a man responsible for the 'crime' of seducing but a woman is not similarly liable. This can be read as the law-saying that women lack sexual agency and thus are not expected to seduce men. Or it could be read as a recognition of the contemporary sexual mores of Indian society where women and men occupy very different power positions and most women are not in a position to 'seduce'. Ved Kumari herself recognises this in the subsequent discussion of provisions dealing with foeticide and infanticide. These provisions are gender neutral in language but they hide and sanitize the social reality that it is only the girl child or female foetus that is intentionally harmed.

She argues that criminal law with regard to rape, marital rape, dowry, etc. has changed in response to the demands by the women's movement but it still incorporates patriarchal values. While she agrees that criminal law needs an exhaustive review she disagrees with the proposal by the National Commission for Women that women should have a separate criminal law. Ved Kumari argues that no doubt gender sensitive laws are required but the entire legal system needs to be gender sensitive rather than segregating women into special areas.

I agree that the reform proposal of the National Commission for Women needs to be challenged. It focuses attention on what kinds of changes are desired by feminists and how may they be achieved. If it is possible to enact segregated gender specific laws, by the same logic the entire legal system could be made gender sensitive. If laws applicable to women are selected and quarantined the mainstream assumptions of the neutrality and universality of law would be left unchallenged. Feminist authors have adequately demonstrated that all knowledge comes from a perspective. It is high time that law scholars accepted that legal knowledge is equally incapable of being a contextual or objective. The main task for legal scholars is to argue that the perspectives adopted in various sites of law are compatible with achieving social justice.

Chandrasekharan Pillai has also discussed some of the criminal law reform proposals of the National Commission for Women and the Law Commission. He has examined the developments in criminal law since the Mathura case. He agrees that lawmakers and administrators must be sensitive to the prevailing social and cultural contexts in which they are applying criminal law but has misgivings about proposals that treat men and women differently. He has analysed the reform proposals for arrest, investigation and trial of women offenders, dowry-related deaths, marital rape and maintenance provisions. In all these areas he acknowledges the specific social context of Indian society but is uncomfortable with the idea of different treatment of men and women. Pillai argues that neutrality or even handedness of law is essential for everyone (and not only women) to have confidence in the system. Thus, proposals that demand that courts or investigation authorities should be only personnel by women work on the wrong presumption that all men are biased against women or all women are pro-women. He argues that crime is essentially a social problem and anyone dealing with that should have the ability to develop sympathetic detachment and appreciate the special nature of the offence.

S.P. Sathe takes a different view than Pillai on the relevance of gender specific law. He has analysed the Supreme Court's changing attitude towards the issue of gender justice. Sathe says that the intensification of women's rights movements all over the world and the international recognition of women's rights as evidenced by CEDAW are some of the factors behind the changes in the Supreme Court's stance towards gender justice. Judges play an important role in the context of a Constitution that provides for a limited government and a bill of rights. It is the judges who must interpret the Constitution to keep in step with the changing social, economic and political circumstances. Thus, the course the Constitutional law takes is very much dependent on the social philosophy and the outlook of the judges.

Sathe analyses the judicial decisions to illustrate how judges share the prevailing societal ideas about gender roles but occasionally they also strive for social change by challenging the prevailing gender roles. The Supreme Court has tried to mainstream the issues of women's rights as human rights by giving a wider interpretation to Article 21 that guarantees personal liberty. The right to privacy is thus extended to women and rape is classified as the violation of a human right—the right to life contained in Article 21. Significantly the Supreme Court has read this right as available against private bodies and individuals as well. Similarly, sexual harassment is treated as the violation of the right to carry on an occupation, right to live with dignity and the right to equality. Sathe however agrees that the Supreme Court has so far failed to uphold the right of women to gender justice when faced with the arguments of freedom of religion, even as Nandita Haksar points to the perils of such intervention.

The judges who manage to transgress the dominant notions of gender roles at the very least show that the law is capable of being understood as a vehicle for change. They also demonstrate the heterogeneity of the meanings of law. However, genuine gender justice demands that the outcome of a case should not depend solely on the individual outlook of the judges. Sathe's article thus makes it abundantly clear that it is important to educate the future judges in a manner that they grasp the interconnections between law and other social institutions.

Sivaramayya has provided an analysis of successive governments' responses to the recommendations of the legal section of the Report of the Committee on the Status of Women (CSW hereafter). He has graphically illustrated the distance between the reform proposals and their actual enactment into law. Sivaramayya analyses the reform proposals on a number of grounds and in the discussion on the Child Marriage Restraint Act related proposals, he shows how the government has either declined to implement the recommendations of the CSW or implemented them partially. As a result, the law is ineffective but this is hardly an inherent incapacity of the law, for the officers appointed to implement the Act are unable to do so because they lack mobility. They are not provided with any transport or transport costs.

Sivaramayya's discussion about the consequences of a child marriage: whether it should be valid or invalid, whether the option of puberty should be available to the woman etc. illustrates the contradictory pulls on law reformers. If they choose to declare a child marriage void they ignore the social reality that the girl/woman whose marriage is declared void will suffer social stigma. So too the consequences flowing for the children of such marriages need to be carefully thought out. What is the real cost of a child marriage and who should pay for it are questions reformers have to answer if women are not to be doubly disadvantaged.

Sivaramayya shows how political will plays a large part in the reform of personal laws. Thus, the central government is loath to abolish the institution of the Mitakshara Joint Hindu Family but various State Legislatures have enacted laws to do so. The judiciary has filled certain important gaps in the Christian personal law but according to Sivaramayya effective social reform requires systematic legislative changes. One of the most significant issues is who should initiate reform.

This issue is illustrated by the problems associated with the reform of 'minority' community's laws and the incapacity of various governments to change the *status quo*. Sivaramayya disagrees with Baxi that minorities need special protection against coercive State action and challenges the idea that minorities should have the right to deny equal rights to women in their communities. He goes further and argues that just as the social justice and welfare measures of the 70s denied equality to women so too the cultural difference and pluralism arguments in the 80s and 90s have served the same purpose.

Sivaramayya's argument makes it obvious that law has to deal with issues of multiplicity and difference in a gender sensitive manner. This issue exemplifies the dilemma of defining what may constitute social justice or non-oppression for women in minority communities. Should the minority women have a voice'? How can their voices be heard unless institutional practices change to accommodate them? This is an issue discussed by Malavika Karlekar and I vill return to it later. Secondly, it needs to be asked whether a stand on any basis, be it religious autonomy, cultural specificity or minority status should be tested on the touchstone of that are the consequences for the concerned women? Nandita Haksar has dealt with this issue in her article. But coming back to the issue of law reform. Alice Jacob has described the intermittent efforts at changing the Christian personal law.

Alice Jacob describes the different points of view about the rightful scope of the proposed clauses on the Uniform Civil Code in the Constitution Assembly Debates. The tension between the scope of a secular personal law and religious personal laws is unresolved even today. The Constitution-makers arrived at a compromise and made the clause on Uniform Civil Code into a directive principle. She argues that the concept of Uniform Civil Code has two aspects: uniformity of law between communities and uniformity of law within communities between the rights of men and women.

Alice Jacob discusses what would constitute a gender just law in the Christian community. She argues that Christian women are entitled to at least the same rights as men. The issue that arises from this argument is whether equality between men and women must mean same rights or can it also encompass the idea that they can have different rights but not contravene the ideal of equality. The distinction between formal and substantive equality is not very well established in most legal scholarship and it is not surprising that this tension is manifest in many articles in this collection as well.

International law has recognised this distinction and there exist many specific conventions that recognise the special needs of women. The principles of international law have percolated into domestic laws in many ways. J.N. Saxena has focussed on International Conventions as a source of human rights for women. Anthony Lester has discussed how developments in international law provided the impetus for transformations in domestic law in the United Kingdom. Neeru Chadha in her article has also illustrated that international conventions are the source of principles of gender justice for domestic law.

J.N. Saxena shows that international law started with gender neutral principles but this discourse has also started acknowledging the need for gender sensitive provisions. He discusses some aspects of the tragedy of dislocation that has affected about ten million refugee women. He argues that of the estimated fifteen million refugees the majority are women yet they have become the concern of the international community only in the last ten to twelve years. Women suffer as do other refugees but they also suffer because of their gender. All too often women have a higher susceptibility to physical abuse and sexual violence before, during and after flight. Saxena describes the development of the concern for women in the international fora. The issues are described as the legal question of determining the refugee status and the issue of dealing with the threat of physical abuse faced by women.

Saxena's article illustrates how gender specificity is important in naming the harms suffered by women because of their gender. This is the first initial step in changing the unsatisfactory state of affairs. The changes contemplated make it clear that the international bodies and law must recognise the agency of women. Women should have a voice in deciding about issues that affect them directly.

Anthony Lester has illustrated the interdependence of national and International law discourse. He has analysed the effect of the European Commission's equal treatment directive on the anti-discrimination law in the United Kingdom. He describes how the domestic law against sex discrimination in the United Kingdom had much narrower scope than the European Commission's Directive. The Equal Opportunity Commission started by interpreting the national legislation in accordance with the Community law. In time the European Court of Justice declared that the United Kingdom's Equal Pay Act failed to give proper effect to the principle of equal pay for work which was different but of equal value.

Anthony Lester argues that the founders of the European Community were motivated by economic as well as social reasons. They wished to avoid any State from gaining an unfair competitive advantage by exploiting women as a cheap source of labour but also wished to promote social progress by constant improvement of living and working conditions. These concerns have however, not extended to forbidding discrimination on other invidious grounds such as colour, race, religion, ethnic or national origins.

Neeru Chadha has similarly discussed the influence of international conventions on the Indian domestic law. She has provided an analysis of the effects of two specific social reform laws, i.e. the Equal Remuneration Act, 1976 and the Maternity Benefit Act, 1961. She argues that the enactment of these statutes leads to the *prima facie* inference that the Indian legal system recognises the special needs of women workers and thus gives them substantive equality. The evidence at the functional level, however, reveals that these provisions do not fulfil the central objective for which they have been enacted.

Neeru Chadha argues that the Equal Remuneration Act establishes an important principle that women and men workers should be paid the same wages for work of same or similar nature. But for a majority of Indian women job segregation means that only women do certain kinds of work, which generally attract low wages. The occupational segregation and wage differentials are not explainable on any rational basis as work done by women is more arduous, requires more energy and women workers have higher productivity rates. Therefore, the fight against ingrained discrimination requires comprehensive schemes of job evaluation. Introduction of the concept of 'comparable worth' could be useful but it is important to supplement this with enhancing the capacity of women workers to access the legal system.

The Maternity Benefit Act has been on the statute-book for a long time but a very low percentage of women workers claim maternity benefits. Many factors are responsible for this state of affairs including the ignorance of women workers about their rights. Trade Unions are generally not supportive of their claims and employers are reluctant to give women workers any maternity benefits. The statutory scheme itself is flawed, as the Act does not prohibit the discharge or dismissal of the pregnant woman. All it says is that if a woman worker is dismissed during pregnancy she can claim maternity benefits.

It is the manifestation of the significance of gender stereotypes that is exhibited in the common responses to the maternity benefits law. The very modest expenditure on maternity benefits does not explain the prevalent perception of individual employers that women workers are more expensive to employ. As a possible way of overcoming this perception various committees have suggested that a central fund for maternity benefits should be created. Each employer should be required to contribute to this fund and thus the perception that the employers of women workers bear an unfair burden can be overcome.

Neeru Chadha argues persuasively that the maternity benefits should not be linked with the government's population control policy. The use of the maternity benefits law as a population control method undermines the idea of maternity benefits as a basic right available to all women. So too the population control measures that penalise women go against the professed aims of the government in various other children and women-related programmes and policies. She argues that the mere availability of rights in statutes carries no meaning and they need to be implemented.

The complexity of achieving social change through state initiated action is also one of the issues discussed by Chhatrapati Singh. He has focussed on the involvement of women in wasteland development in India and analysed the forestry lams in India in general and Himachal Pradesh in particular. He illustrates that in most cases the ownership and/or usufruct fights are given to the male head of family. Even if sometimes women are given usufruct rights they still fail to gain equality as the other general civil and personal laws governing property relationships deny them property rights. In this context of disparity of property rights women's reliance on their labour has severe limitations.

The systematic discrimination is maintained as forestry work is usually neither classified as agricultural sector or industrial and is unorganised. As a result, the limited protection of various labour laws is unavailable to the forestry workers. But even where forestry work is classified as agricultural work and the Minimum Wages Act, 1948 applies, women's work is classified as unskilled or semi-skilled and they are paid less. So too when labour rules under the Forest Act 1927 are applied women are still classified as doing 'soft' work and paid less. The Minimum Wages Act provides an elaborate administrative machinery but even then the implementation of the Act is dismal.

Chhatrapati Singh argues that for democratic institutional processes to develop it is essential that grass-roots involvement of people is facilitated. This may be done either by supporting the Panchayats or by organising people into legally recognised structures like many non-government organisations (NGOs). The legal form and status of an association is important and it has implications for the management of resources. So too the resource utilisation policies must be informed by the concerns of the local peoples. Chhatrapati Singh has demonstrated eloquently the need for a holistic approach to the issue of the regeneration of wastelands. He has established that changes are required not only in the forest and land laws but also in the Panchayat Acts, labour laws, family laws and property laws.

Echoes of the same idea that is the need for a multi-pronged approach to achieve change through law is present in the arguments of S. Muralidhar. He has provided graphic details of the saga of the Agra Home case. This case illustrates the complexity of relying on public interest litigation (PIL) to make the authorities accountable under the law. S. Muralidhar has demonstrated how the coordination between various institutions of the State is essential for the effective implementation of social welfare legislation. The commitment of the petitioners and the efforts of the Supreme Court to introduce a semblance of accountability in the administration of the Agra Home are negated again and again by insufficient resources for effective enforcement of court orders. The Supreme Court ultimately decided to hand over the Home matter to the National Human Rights Commission but it has played a pivotal role in accepting the petition and following it up to an extent. The step by step account of the developments makes for disheartening reading but S. Muralidhar is not suggesting that instituting the proceedings was a futile exercise. The changes achieved are less than adequate but the non-involvement of the Supreme Court does not present itself as an option.

The contradictions in relying on a less than perfect and patriarchal legal system to obtain justice for men is well illustrated by the story of Agra Home. The same tension is present in S. Muralidhar's analysis of the legal regulation of prostitution. He analyses the draconian provisions in the Immoral Traffic Prevention Act, 1956 and demonstrates that they are consistently used to the detriment of women prostitutes. Yet he is not sure that abolishing all legal regulation of prostitution is the answer to the problem, as issues arising from child prostitution need to be addressed. So too the children of prostitute women deserve more attention and care. S. Muralidhar concludes that the PIL concerning the Agra Home has provided many possibilities of inter-disciplinary collaborative efforts for tackling the complex web of law and poverty.

The Indian Supreme Court has played an important role in the development of PIL, which has provided the only avenue of safeguarding human rights of many vulnerable sections of society. However, Upendra Baxi and Nandita Haksar have questioned this reliance on the human rights discourse. They have analysed the human rights discourse from two different perspectives and analysed the complexity of changing the legal discourse. Unlike Chhatrapati Singh they are more ambivalent about the power of law to achieve meaningful social transformation.

Nandita Haksar acknowledges the complexities in relying on the human rights discourse. She focuses on the conflict between feminist and civil rights perspectives and describes how the debates in the feminist movement and the human rights movement often took place in ignorance of each other.

She says that the efforts for developing feminist and human rights jurisprudence must be understood in the contexts in which these re-definitions happened. Thus, the feminists challenged the taken for granted rule that a lawyer must accept any brief and by refusing to represent the accused in rape trials they helped bring into focus the disadvantages faced by a rape victim. However, the conflict between human rights and feminist ethics remains as is illustrated by this example. She suggests that all lawyers and not only feminist or civil libertarian lawyers make choices. She puts to rest the notion that lawyers can be neutral with the astute observation that a human rights lawyer provides solidarity while a *pro bono* lawyer provides charity and there is a vast difference between the two.

Nandita Haksar draws out the complexities of feminists' engagement with law reform and shows how the women's movement's demand for an in-camera trial of rape cases was recommended by the Law Commission with the justification that it will provide protection to the accused man as well. This example illustrates how the significance of gender hierarchies is lost on our policy-makers because very often they accept formal parity as the only legitimate interpretation of equality. Moreover, the demands for in-camera trials and closed court were received with mixed feelings by various women's organisations. On the one hand these changes could be of some help to the woman complainant but on the other hand the same provisions could justify censorship and prevent women's movement from publicising violence against women. Similarly, there is a tension in women's movement's response to the law of obscenity: it is very often used as a means of delegitimising dissent against abuse of power but feminists also wished to pin responsibility on those using the cover of freedom of speech argument to publish anti-women writing. The efforts of feminists to distinguish between pornography and obscenity have floundered once again partly because of the inability of the decision-makers to recognise the gender specificity of the harm of pornography for women.

Nandita Haksar argues that the ready acceptance of the dichotomy between individual rights and the rights of minorities resulted in the easy sacrifice of vital civil and political rights. She believes that rather than accepting the Liberal paradigm of rights the Indian feminists should produce a critique of law so as to evolve a new jurisprudence. She illustrates this issue very convincingly with the example of women's movement's responses to the north-east 'tribal' women's relationship to their traditional laws. She argues that change must come through a broad-based social movement and it is only when the movement is strong enough to carry the law reform forward that legal battles become relevant.

Upendra Baxi has utilised the story of Kamla to analyse the issues in relation to sex trafficking as an instance of human rights violations of women sex workers. He argues that the scholar community in India has failed to analyse various consequences of sex trafficking. Moreover, the deployment of human rights discourse is problematic for various reasons. The fact that after Kamla's disappearance prosecutorial discretion was used to impose a total silence on human rights discourse is not an unsurprising example of how law, policy and administration combine to sustain regimes of patriarchy. In the case of Kamla recourse to the language of human rights brings out the crucial fact that the law and the State are not neutral sites of redressing injury but wield power to injure. He goes on to suggest that the contemporary formulations of human rights are inadequate and that adequate formulations will enshrine the right of Indian women to be and remain women.

Upendra Baxi argues that a mere assertion of human rights without challenging the relations of social production can only be harmful. His contention is that there is a need for renaming the human rights praxis as the market for human rights-akin to markets in other commodities. His other major contention is that the task of fashioning of solidarity and collective rights of those forced into sexual trafficking require a paradigmatic shift from the languages of human rights to those of human solidarity. Various possible strategies of engaging with human rights issues ultimately empower the human rights communities and conscientious public actors but what is really needed is the emergence of the politics of the violated. And even though contemporary psychoanalytic and post-modernist approaches quibble over what does it mean to be a woman Upendra Baxi argues for a corporeal (justice-in-the-flesh) notion of justice.

Upendra Baxi makes a crucial argument about the need for a paradigmatic shift in thinking about rights. Such a shift can occur only if the nature of legal knowledge is questioned. The notions of objectivity and neutrality of legal principles need to be constantly challenged and one way of doing this is to make the study of law a truly inter-disciplinary study. Archana Parashar has discussed the need for inter-disciplinary study of law. She argues that feminist analyses of law are often seen as special interests of some feminists but they need to be understood as challenging the fundamental conception of legal knowledge. The rise of post-structural theory provides the paradigmatic shift as it challenges the idea of objective knowledge and legal knowledge can not be an exception to this development. There is ample legal literature in this genre but most legal education is still organised around the study of legal doctrine.

There is a sad lack of inter-disciplinarity in most contemporary Indian legal scholarship. Malavika Karlekar's article is therefore a welcome illustration of the possibilities. She has provided a study of widowhood in nineteenth century Bengal. She has used the literary genre to illustrate the experiences of widowhood by analysing the story of Nistarini Debi. Malavika Karlekar discusses the reform processes that lead to the enactment of the Hindu Women's Remarriage Act, 1856. She discusses the role played by various reformers who were in part informed by women suffering from the social customs associated with widowhood. Different reformers targeted different methods of reform. In addition to law reform they relied on social activism, educated women and published a journal for women as well as wrote poetry and stories on topics like polygamy.

Malavika Karlekar uses Nistarini Debi's story to illustrate the resilience of a woman battling the unfair, materialistic marriage rules and observances. This first-hand account intermeshes social history and tradition with actual experiences and thus yields powerful messages about the social conditions of widowed women. She argues that Nistarini Debi is able to convey her resistance even in the limiting confines of Kuhn widowhood and thereby give a voice to those among the most oppressed.

This kind of knowledge has to be relevant for every lawyer and lawmaker. Yet in most law curricula this kind of literature finds no place. This argument links up with Amita Dhanda's argument that it is important to recognise the resistance offered by women for what it is. All too often women are portrayed as the victims and the reforms are seen as paternalistic concern of some men for helpless women. While it is true that very often legal change required (and still does) the input of men reformers, it is also worth remembering that women have found ways of resisting and exercising their sense of agency. This issue is brought out with elegance in Vina Mazumdar's discussion of political reservations for women. The judges play an important role in constructing and legitimising ideas about appropriate social roles for women but manage to distance themselves from these ideas by relying on the notions of objective legal knowledge. Usha Ramanathan has effectively challenged such claims by documenting the process of construction of legal knowledge by the judges.

Amita Dhanda has analysed the power exercised by judges in psychologising the dissent of women. She argues that movement for change in the dominant norms begins through dissent but change in fact occurs only if dissent is accepted as dissent. One obvious strategy for stalling change is to classify dissent as socially undesirable behaviour. She uses the concept of psychologising to demonstrate how dissent by married women is not accepted as their legitimate protest against a subsisting reality but is transformed into a reaction of the troubled mind of the dissenters. The issue therefore becomes a problem of the individual rather than that of the institution, community, or society. Judicial psychologising is even more sinister as it leads to legal entrenchment of social attitudes towards women at the very least by the 'captive audiences' that are the compulsory consumers of judgments, i.e. law students, lawyers, future judges. It also results in making role stereotypes an unquestioned and integral part of legal reality. Such psychologising results in denial of rights to the dissenters.

Amita Dhanda argues that there is a need for psychiatrists to appreciate the non-medical objectives that are very often attempted to be achieved through psychiatric detentions. The legislature has acknowledged the possibility that a person may need psychiatric treatment but not institutional psychiatric treatment. The judiciary is however, yet to accept this notion. Amita Dhanda argues that psychiatric detentions can often be used as a measure of social control to manage institutional discipline and departures from role stereotypes. Judicial officers can play a significant role in safeguarding the rights of the mentally ill but for this they must learn not to rely mechanically on the perceptions of doctors, family or community.

Usha Ramanathan, however, dampens this optimism with her examination of judicial pronouncements regarding appropriate behaviour for women and men. She argues that judges construct differently the notions of reasonable woman and reasonable man. Even though the idea that reasonable man is a suspect concept is well established in feminist legal scholarship, it is not as yet extensively illustrated in Indian legal research.

Moreover, she has not confined herself to usual areas associated with gender analysis. Instead she has collected judicial pronouncements across a very wide spectrum and demonstrated that all areas of law are significant for women. At the very least it challenges the notion that only some areas of law need to be gender specific or gender sensitive.

Usha Ramanathan has illustrated graphically the construction of legal knowledge by the judges. For example, she shows how the jurisprudence of the husband's right to beat his wife is constructed. Similarly, with regard to maintenance she shows how judges have drawn peremptory standards women must live up to if they wish to receive maintenance. Judges have attributed differential although equally arbitrary value to the 'loss' of a wife in cases of adultery. She brings out the striking fact that women are denied any agency and are treated as the property of men.

The kind of primary data collected by Usha Ramanathan is a significant and very accessible research resource available for further inter-disciplinary analyses by feminist scholars. It is important for legal scholars to broaden their analyses of law but it is equally important for scholars in other disciplines to understand law in its broadest dimensions. Women's movement in India has shown a spectrum of attitudes towards law but very often the understanding of law is not adequate.

Vina Mazumdar has provided an insider's view of the ambivalence of the Indian women's movement towards the law. She starts by acknowledging that the diversity in the women's movement is also reflected in the multiplicity of attitudes towards law-making. However, she argues that the diverse and charging attitudes to law are not evidence of contradictions but reflect the interdependence of women's demands and historical developments. She argues that the changes in the political, social, economic and other national realities have affected the positions adopted by women's movement. Mazumdar illustrates her argument with a study of three issues: identity politics and women's movement; violence against women; and political representation.

She has provided a rare history of the Indian women's movement and explained how in the 1970s and 1980s Indian feminist scholars and activists began a process to redefine what are women's issues in the Indian context. Most notably the Indian women's movement chose to concern itself with the problems, perspectives and priorities of the majority of women and broadened its base by listening to women who had remained invisible to the elite—both men and women.

The women's movement has neither accepted the theology of free market nor of globalisation but has insisted on the government's responsibility as India is a welfare State. Yet the women's movement is yet to resolve the issue of how to protect the rights of minorities in general and at the same time achieve human rights. Minority communities often feel threatened by cultural and ethnic extinction and tend to adopt regressive attitudes towards their women's basic freedoms and customary rights. She acknowledges that secularism *per se* cannot ensure social development for all of India's communities.

Vina Mazumdar eloquently describes her disenchantment with the law in delivering gender justice for women but she can still argue that a historical failure at a particular point of time should not be generalised to a point of universalisation as an impossibility. Thus, her description of women's movement's role in getting rape laws modified demonstrates the role of lay people in mobilising public opinion to force the government of the day to act. The modified rape laws have not significantly affected the incidence of rape but it is important to recognise that is so because the enforcement continues to be poor. The campaign for rape law reform had another consequence as it generated ideological unanimity in the women's movement to assist poorer women in empowering themselves to oppose violence against women, to oppose growing communalism and fundamentalist violence, or the use of violence against women as an instrument of political action. She argues that disagreements, however, remain with regard to dowry-related violence: whether the efforts should be directed at preventive measures or on retributive measures. The changes in crimnal law have been introduced but women's movement has been unable to improve the enforcement of these laws or reduce the incidence of violence against women. Many in the women's movement accept that legal changes must be accompanied with empowering the women to change their attitudes so that social norms can be challenged along with legal norms.

Vina Mazumdar argues that "there is a general tendency amongst feminist scholars to blame the biased judiciary or the patriarchal State. Such analyses take a simplistic view of the legal system and ignore the obvious fact that just like any other functions of the government the legal process is a complex function. In order to understand the significance of various factors the entire legal system must be examined." The women's movement has failed to contextualise the rising rate of violence against women and so the blame on the law ignores the socio-political pathology and the failure of social controls.

She describes how the efforts by the national government to introduce Constitutional amendments penalising those contravening the two-child policy were halted at a late stage because the National Commission for Women's Act required consultation with the National Commission for Women. This is a good illustration of how at times the State-enacted laws can act as a check on itself. She criticises the position of some feminists that rights and justice are abstract concepts and argues that Indian scholars do not recognise the evolutionary nature of these concepts within Indian culture and history. Amongst other things the role that legal education has played in shaping the culture and biases of the entire legal profession remains unanalysed. Archana Parashar takes up the issue of the role of legal education in changing the contemporary understandings of the law.

In last, it can be concluded, Archana Parashar finds problematic the Indian women movement's disillusionment with law. She notes a shift in the movement from seeking normative change to obtaining a greater share of existing services for women. This approach may obtain greater services for women but it would not address the normative inadequacies of existing structures. Without such interrogation social justice would remain an elusive goal. In order to address the normative inadequacies of the legal system Archana Parashar asks for a feminist reconceptualisation of legal education. Legal feminism she holds should form an integral part of legal education.

II. GENDER DIMENSION

AMITA DHANDA

The book was being organised around the argument that if the gender dimensions of law were to be understood and explored then such an exploration could not be confined to family law and women specific provisions of criminal law, it had to permeate to all areas of the law.

The need to strengthen and nurture our institutions is often spoken of without realising that the primary unit of any institution is the individual. In order to build the institution the individuals in it have to be nurtured. Finding the time to listen to another's personal or professional difficulties, applauding a good effort, pointing out an error without undermining the person are all aspects of nurturance.[21]

Furthermore, I think the issue of gender is viewed and understood from a variety of perspectives. These diverse views definitely occupy spaces of the mind but do not enter the public domain because of the academic inhibition to voice opinions on issues outside subject specialisations. 'Mindsets can be changed' only if what is in the mind can be said. Every shade of opinion from the conservative to the liberal to the radical finds representation in the collection.

---

21. The Manu Sabha was a group that the students at the Faculty of Law, Delhi set up. Every week any one member made an academic presentation to which the others reacted. Membership was restricted and student controlled. The teacher coordinators—Prof. Sarkar and Mr. Narasimhaswamy G. Mysore—were also chosen by the students. Manu Sabha, Dr. Sarkar holds was real democracy. She describes the five-year period for which the Sabha ran as the most enjoyable and rewarding ones of her life. Appropriately, Surendra Malik, the publisher of this book was a member of this Manu Sabha.

Whilst concerns of gender are primarily voiced in relation to the situation of women in law, articulations on male stereotyping are not absent.

Archana Parashar makes a case for problematising such stereotyping. Ved Kumari voices concern for the male victim and Usha Ramanathan shows how through the construct of the reasonable man a number of societal preconceptions are accorded legitimacy in law. A stereotyping process, which even if less disadvantageous for men, is surely no less restricting as it reduces for men the opportunities to differ from it.

For the women, stereotyping has robbed away the attributes of a thinking, feeling and doing human. It is only a thing which does not think, feel and act by her own choice. This process of thingification which extends to her commodification has been severely interrogated by Upendra Baxi. A significant strategy to undermine if not reverse this process of commodification is to give voice to the feelings and desires of women. For a thing may be a desirable object and could be desired but she herself cannot desire.

Voice has been given to the aspirations, feelings, desires of women in a number of essays in this collection. Malavika Karlekar's exegesis on Kuhn widowhood is not only about the plight of widows in Bengal, it is also an expression of the needs, feelings and desires of Nistarini Debi, her trials and tribulations as she attempts to salvage her dignity from within the role requirements of widowhood. Subsumed within the legal category of reasonable woman, is the woman. This woman is the sub-text of Usha Ramanathan's article. Even as she presents how courts dealt with issues relating to women, she tells us of the married woman who desires not her husbands forgiveness but an opportunity to live life on her own terms,[22] of the young revolutionary who in consonance with her political choices prefers punishment to pardon.[23]

Muralidhar's saga of the Agra Protective Home is not

---

22. Gahra *v.* Emperor, AIR 1926 Lab 176.
23. Emperor *v.* Kamal Dattatraya Sohoni, AIR 1943 Bom 304.

only about the court case, it is also about the inmates of the protective home, their life aspirations and frustrations with their place of protection. It is about women needing places of refuge whilst they aspire to establish identities of their own. It is this quest for an identity which caused Lalita to fight right up to the Supreme Court against an incorrect description of her.[24] Most importantly it is about an intrepid petitioner who carried on the struggle to seek constitutional rights for the inmates of the Agra Protective Home both with and without her co-petitioner.

It is this capacity to stand alone, to differ if she cannot agree, and the ability to refuse prestigious offers such as membership of the Law Commission if it meant compromising on her values—in short her courage to dissent—which caused me to focus on the value of dissent in a volume on Lotika Sarkar. My piece again whilst narrating efforts to subjugate dissent also brings to the fore women who refused to turn a blind eye to unjust situations.

A stereotype like an opinion can be interrogated only if material contesting it is available. The above-mentioned essays provide unimpeachable evidence of the availability of such material. It seems imperative that legal research does not just analyse legislative norms and their judicial interpretation but also starts to bring to the fore those meanings which the users of the law wish to be adopted. Some insights on this aspect can be obtained on the legislative front from the evidences and memoranda before parliamentary and other law reform committees and on the adjudicative front from activation patterns, fact narration and litigant profiles. On autopoetic logic[25] if the minds of legislators and judges are to be changed then the countering efforts should be inaugurated from within the legal system.

Such an exercise we hope would be undertaken even for the areas covered by the volume. Thus, Ved Kumari and

23. Emperor *v.* Kamal Dattatraya Sohoni, AIR 1943 Bom 304.
24. Lalita's Cease SLP (Cri) No. 161/1986.
25. Fritjof Capra, The Web of Life: A New Synthesis of Mind and Matter, Flamingo, London, 1997.

Pillai have undertaken a detailed analysis of the legislative norms in substantive and procedural criminal law impact on women. Both articles however focus on women as victims. Women figure in the criminal justice system not just as complainants but also as accused persons and witnesses. It may be worthwhile to ask would our philosophy of criminal prosecution alter if the accused person is a woman—illustratively women engaged in drug running or petty crime. Such querying may induct into law-making the Gandhian talisman, of keeping in view the most vulnerable person you know, an exercise surely in the interest of all vulnerables.

On the testimonial front, do women witnesses encounter any special difficulties as witnesses. Whilst investigating the conditions of persons with mental illness in the jails of West Bengal we (Dr. Srinivasa Murthy and myself) encountered a number of rape victims who had been kept in custody for rendering testimony in their cases even as the accused persons had been released on bail.[26] The ostensible reason proffered for such detention was the travelling difficulties encountered by these women. In a similar vein, especially in the light of the recent hysterectomy controversy, it would be pertinent to find out what do the police do when the complainant of rape or sexual assault or kidnapping is a woman with mental disability?

To seek an answer to this query it would become necessary to find out what the law is, not just as the Supreme Court of India says it is, but also as the station house officer, judicial magistrate and sessions judge declare it to be. It is true that in accordance with legal doctrine the decisions of the Supreme Court of India are the law of the land and that of the State High Court the law of the State, but for an individual citizen the law very often is what the local policeman says it is.

Legal research would need to view as its field of study not just legislation's, appellate court decisions but also rules, practices, policies and schemes.

---

26. Unlock the Padlock Menial Health Care in West Bengal, Report of the Supreme Court Commission on Mentally Ill in the Jails of West Bengal, 1993.

Even as appellate court decisions are being studied it may be worthwhile to not only ponder on the cases which reach the court but also on those which are either not filed or do not make the grade. Thus, D.N. Saraf in his piece on consumer protection informs us of the medical negligence cases filed by women. The cases in Saraf's collection cause one to wonder as to why despite the tall claims made in advertisements for cosmetics and the number of beauty advises on failed beauty care sought in newspaper columns, beauticians and cosmetic manufacturers have not been hauled up before consumer courts. Is it because it is easier for a woman to complain of inadequate obstretic than beauty services? Is the myth of the beautiful woman a strategy in aid of unregulated commerce?[27]

Archana Parashar in her piece on feminism in legal education makes a strong case for inducting feminism into legal education. This she holds is imperative if the goal of social justice which is the *raison d'etre* of law is to be achieved. Archana Parashar advocates for a foundational reordering of legal education. The U.G.C. Legal Curriculum Committee whilst considering the question of gender in the undergraduate law course, opted one for a special paper on women and law[28] and two, asked for gender dimensions to be explored in each area of law.

Discussing this recommendation with Dr. Sarkar, Archana and I expressed the apprehension that a special paper on Women and Law would ghettoise gender and except for those students who opted for the paper, the rest would graduate uninitiated from law school. The special paper she told us was opted for because it was feared that if gender was introduced only as part of a paper then upon pressure of time it may be the first segment which may get dropped.

---

27. Naomi Woolf, The Beauty Myth: How images of beauty are used against women, William Morrow and Company Inc., New York, 1991.

28. Report of the Curriculum Development Centre in Law, University Grants Commission, New Delhi, 1992, pp. 180-83.

Later whilst coordinating a course on feminism in legal education at Trivandrum in 1996, Archana and I encountered at first-hand resistance to the idea of restructuring law courses on the strength of feminist principles. Feminism we were told could be taught as one more school of jurisprudence. Inducting notions of gender into legal education did not require a restructured syllabi but only a gender sensitive teacher. Furthermore, every area of law did not have a gender dimension, therefore, a foundational reordering of the legal curriculum was not in order.

The fact that all teachers are not gender sensitive and that instruments to sensitise them are required was not considered. And, can it be said that there are areas of law which cannot be feminised: the law of taxation, or contracts or corporations.

It is this presumption which causes the Fifth Pay Commission to recommend that part time work options may be created for women workers to aid the due fulfilment of their child rearing responsibilities.[29] For if family caring responsibilities are responsibilities of all workers and not women workers alone then strategies to restructure rather than level the workplace would be required. A foundational interrogation of fixed hours of work, night work, double shifts as work organization options would be needed.

A feminist teaching of the law of taxation would raise questions on what constitutes income? What is the value of house work? Should housework be monetised for tax purposes and income from it clubbed with that of the outside work Income along with joint ownership of the savings made to obtain rebate. A trenchant criticism the Chelliah Committee has made of direct taxes statutes is that too many social purposes were attempted to be obtained through the tax laws making for a complicated and inefficient tax system.[30] Whether or not was criticism can be extended to gender-

29. Report of the Fifth Central Pay Commission, Ministry of Finance, Government of India, Vol. III, Jan. 1997, p. 1713.
30. Tax Reforms Committee, Final Report, Ministry of Finance, Government of India, Part I, 1992, pp. 3-4.

based tax reforms, the deconstruction of basic tax concepts shows the extent to which they reinforce the existing public-private divide. Similar questions could be raised in the realm of corporations and contracts.

A major issue confronted by the Indian women's movement which is dwelled on at some length by Vina Mazumdar in her piece relates to the efficacy of law as a vehicle of social change. This query is often asked without appreciating that if legal regulation of an area is already in place then engagement with law is not a matter of choice. The choicelessness of the situation emerges all the more sharply when the everyday form of law, i.e. rules, orders, notifications and forms are examined from a feminist perspective. I am referring to encounters with subordinate legislation as choiceless because they occur during efforts to organise everyday life be it to obtain a ration card, seek admission in college, admit your child in school or obtain a passport. The forms that have to be filled mechanically seek information on the marital status and parentage of the applicant. These exercises routinely undermine the independent identity of a woman and align it with that of her father or husband.

It was the Indian Foreign Service Rules which required a woman in the foreign service to seek government permission before she got married. And again regulations of the Indian Airlines which provided that an airhostess would lose her job upon pregnancy. The existence of rules of such kind as also their discriminatory character came to light only when they were judicially challenged.[31] Prior to the court decision they were followed by women officers in the IFS and by airhostesses respectively as law. This all pervasive character of subordinate legislation underscores the inevitability of engaging with law and also shows that the discrimination inflicted by this form of law cannot be unearthed through individual enterprise but has necessarily to be an institutional effort.

---

31. C.B. Muthamma *v.* Union of India (1979) 4 SCC 260 and Air India International *v.* Nargesh Meerza (1981) 4 SCC 335.

The volume also shows how the various actors of the legal system make choices. Whilst Nandita Haksar and Muralidhar delineate the choices lawyers make in the cases they take up and the arguments they proffer. Usha Ramanathan and S.P. Sathe elaborate on the influence of individual predilection in adjudication. Whilst these essays blow the cover from the neutrality claims of law, they also underscore the need to research on the choices made by other players of the legal system be it the police, the prosecutor or the academic. The last we hold important because it is what the legal scholar chooses to research and what the law teacher chooses to teach that could in great measure influence what the law makers choose to think.

2

Why Reasonable Man Only?

Usha Ramanathan

I

The "reasonable man" is a product of English, judicial, genius.[1] He was created for justicing convenience. Judges, attempting to unravel the mysteries of human conduct, intent and motive, have for years turned to the Reasonable Man for

1. The reasonable man was characterised by Lord Bowen as "the man on the Clapham Omnibus", and so cited by Lord Greer L.J. in Hall *v.* Brooklands Auto Racing Club (1933) 1 KB 205 at 224. An American writer, also quoted by Lord Greer L.I. in Hall. described him as "the man who takes the magazines at home, and in the evening pushes the lawmover in his shirt sleeves." Eldredge, Modern Ton Problems is quoted as saying, "The reasonable man is a fiction—he is the personification of the court and jury's social judgment." And, as Lord Macmillan would say, the judge has to decide what "reasonable" means, and it is inevitable that different judges may take valiant views on the same question with respect to such an elastic term: Glasgow Corporation *v.* Muir, 1943 AC 448 at 457 see W.V.H. Rogers, Winfield and Jolowicz on Tort, Sweet and Maxwell, London, (Thirteenth edn.), 1989, pp. 46-47.

   Rogers adds a comment: "Despite the inveterate use of the masculine gender, there is no doubt that the personification includes the reasonable woman", p. 46, fn 32. We may of course arrive at a different conclusion.

guidance. Defiance and delinquency have been determined by reference to him. The choice between condemnation and compassion have rested on judicial expectations of what a Reasonable Man would have done.

Madam Usha Ramanathan has discussed vividly. She said that, of course the assumptions in defining the Reasonable Man beg to be challenged. This generalisation, upon manufacture, takes on the mask of principle, dislocates the particularity of the individual and is pragmatic without pretense of perfection. The judicial function, being in large measure a matter of relating the broad statements of enacted law to individual contexts and acts or omissions, this generalisation which displaces difference and produces stereotypes is particularly suspect.

The presence of the Reasonable Man, however, alerts us to the possible existence of the Reasonable Woman. The phrase was never enunciated, perhaps because judges followed the fashion of the day where legislators, clubbed women, minors and the mentally incapable together, as being deficient in reason. Perhaps it was the recognition of proprietorship of the man over woman, which rendered reference to her reason irrelevant. Or, again, perhaps it was the relative rarity of women accessing courts which made her a player around whom cases were fought, but who was not bidden to contribute her perspective to the few principles that developed in her name.

Yet, it must be said, the presence of women in law reports is not limited, either in its frequency or in its variety, to cases where women moved the courts. As accused, as victim, as witness and as property, women have been drawn into courts, and pronounced upon.

Revisiting the decisions of High Courts between 1920 and 1950 introduces us to a triumvirate of judicial creations: the Reasonable Woman, the Reasonable Man and Reasonable Expectations.[2]

2. The source for the cases is the decisions reported in the All India Reporter from 1920 to 1950. It includes decisions from all High Courts, as also from the Privy Council and the Federal Court. All judgments where women were featured and spoken about were extracted. What was largely left out were decisions under the

II

Women, these cases tell us, are essentially of three kinds. There is the wife. The wife who is wronged by the husband; the wife who drives her husband to desperation; the wife who is seduced by another: the wife who is slandered. There is empathy for the cause of paying a price to become a wife, as there is derisive ire poured on those who murderously lead a wife to the pyre of her husband. Occasionally, the wife is replaced by the mother or the daughter.

Then there is the non-wife. In her relationship with a man, she is recognised as possessing an autonomy and independence which is not granted to the wife. Sometimes identified as a concubine, at others as a prostitute, there is an agency which is acknowledged in the non-wife which is quite categorically denied to the wife. She is her own person, and not the creation and concern of a 'guardian'. We also meet the woman in prostitution who challenges the power of the state to exile her from her home.

In a third projection, she is the criminal. There is the cold, callous criminal who kills children to steal their ornaments. She is sent off, with equal coldness, to the death row. And there is the victim of passion who, in attempting to hide her illegitimate infant from life itself, impels the judges to plead for executive clemency.

Sometimes prominently, sometimes in interstices, the Reasonable Man and Reasonable Expectations appear in these narratives.

III

Marriage provides a good starting point for telling tales.

---

categories of Hindu law, Mahomedan law, Parsi law . . . except for a few illustrative cases on marriage, maintenance and divorce. The reason for leaving them out was that they inhabit a universe in which familial hierarchies and property relationships are at its centre, and its politics could be better explored in a work on personal laws.

A woman derives spiritual benefit in gifting property to her son-in-law in consideration of his marrying her daughter.[3] The message from the court was unequivocal. The context was provided by reversioners who battled gallantly to retrieve property that the woman had let pass from the hands of the family to a relative stranger.[4] They lost, but a lot was said before the case was through.

A profile of the dutiful widow and her property emerges from amidst a profusion of precedents and allusions to ancestral texts. Being without male issue, the court said, there was no denying that the lady in question had succeeded to her husband's property as an absolute owner. Yet, her power of disposition was qualified. It was apparent to the court that a wife who survives her husband and takes the entire estate of her husband is enjoined to perform acts which are to increase the prosperity of her and her lord, such as, performing sraddhas, digging wells, etc., and giving presents with pious liberality in proportion to the wealth inherited by her. It is not to be forgot that it is "the performance of religious and charitable purposes and acts conducive to the welfare of the husband (which) are the objects for which she takes the estate of her husband." For, ills o be remembered that "(m)aking useless gifts to dancers, players and the like and the wearing of delicate apparel, etc., the tasting of rich food, etc. and the like being improper for a widow who is enjoined to restrain her passions (they) are equal to theft." The distinction between "legal necessity for worldly purposes" and "the promotion of spiritual benefit of the deceased" would determine the limits of the widow's

3. Ram Sumran Prasad *v.* Govind Dos, AIR 1926 Pat 582 (Jwala Prasad and Bucknill, JJ.).

4. An aside before we set off: it is impressive, the range of issues that reach courts as squabbles over property rights. "Reversioners"—those to whom property reverts after the lifetime of a person who inherits partially as do, for instance, widows who are only given a life estate—have contributed a rich fund of cases in their pursuit of inheritances. To illustrate, validity of marriages, sanity of erstwhile holders of property, *bona fides* of guardians have often been called into question out of a distant, and often obscure, past. See also, for e.g., Ram Sumran, *supra* n. 3.

power of disposition. And ancient wisdom joins a widow not to commit "waste" and "prohibit(s) expenditure not useful or beneficial to the late owner of the property."[5]

Where, then, does the gift to the son-in-law come in? First of all, the widow was performing an "imperative and religious duty" when she arranged for her daughter's marriage. It was also plain that had she not agreed to giving the property to her son-in-law, the marriage would have never happened. The mother, anxious to seal the match, would then have had her wishes thwarted. Moreover, a gift of land to a son-in-law on the occasion of marriage or at the time of departure (bidai) is meritorious, and the gift can be made at the time of the actual marriage or in connection with the ceremonies connected with it.[6]

The gift of landed property was, according to the court[7] on this reasoning a reasonable expectation, lending legitimacy to the widow's power to alienate property—a power denied to her in almost every other circumstance.

We may pause at another court which tells us that "purchase of a woman" by "payment of a ...sum" to "secure a wife" was customary in the community of the marrying man, and "the transaction was not really in the nature of a 'purchase' in the sense urged."[8]

And move on.

The economics of marriage notwithstanding, Hindu law, the courts would say, regards marriage as a sacrament constituting a holy and indissoluble union, primarily for the propagation of children, and also to ensure the performance of certain religious duties.[9] Dissolving the indissoluble requires both judicial will and textual support. Manu Smriti, Yagnyavalkya Smriti and Narada Smriti are illustrative, and capable, assistants to judicial sophistry. They may be read to assert the inevitability, and customary correctness, of the

---

5. *Supra* n. 3.
6. *Ibid.*
7. *Ibid.*
8. Bhan Singh *v.* Rain Singh, AIR 1931 Lah 599 (Bhide J.).
9. Smt. Ratan Moni Debi *v.* Nagendra Narain Singh, AIR 1949 Cal 404 (Edgley J.).

bribing of bridegrooms.[10] Or, with deftness, they may be selectively interpreted as anachronisms.

So it came to pass that a proposition that impotence ought not to make marriage dissoluble since niyoga was a substitute of some vintage met with English judge's metaphorical curling of the nose. It led to his finding authorities that declared the obsolescence of niyoga, even as he declared that a matrimonial alliance between an ordinary healths' woman and an impotent man as an indissoluble union was contrary to public policy. The marriage was annulled.[11]

Divorce does not, however, deserve the support that marriage does. And it certainly is not legal necessity when a mother sells property to find the resources to obtain her daughter's divorce. The daughter's claim to a share in her mother's property, as reversioner and made long years after its sale, was rejected by the court, but not before the court iterated its position that "under the Hindu law, no doubt, the marriage of a daughter would be a legal necessity justifying the alienation of property by a widow. A divorce. however, is against the policy of Hindu law, and no precedent has been pointed out which would justify the court in holding that a divorce may be regarded as a legal necessity."[12]

Resistance to divorce is expressed in other ways too, as where the court would say: "No one can demand a divorce as of right, nor yet a declaration of nullity." The status that marriage confers, and the consequences that flow from it, "particularly after consummation are so serious and far-reaching, especially with regard to the children of the marriage, that any breaking up of the marriage tie cannot be left to the choice of the individual." It is therefore that, in divorce proceedings, the discretion of the court "is absolute. There is no question of limitation. There is no question of estoppel. There is no question of laches. . . . (T)hese are not

---

10. See *supra* n. 3.
11. *Supra* n. 9.
12. Tange'a Venkappa *v.* Goindappa Avappa, AIR 1928 Bom 495 (Fawcett Ag. CJ and Mirza J.).

ordinary civil proceedings. They are matters in which the state is interested and are matters in which the courts can, and must, make as full and complete an investigation as they can."[13]

Again, "the state is vitally concerned in the institution of marriage and insists on strict proof and a close investigation before it will permit the tie to be dissolved." It is extreme and "very rare" cases, "always (for) adequate reasons", which may justify a deviation from the norm of holding marriages together by law.[14]

It is in a matter concerning "unwifely" conduct that the uneven effect of the difficulty of divorce was suggested. The court, in passing, referred to the society where the husband may marry more wives than one, and "the woman has no such corresponding privilege", nor can she obtain a divorce, "for divorce in this community is not recognised."[15]

Now to the unwifely conduct. The wife initiated a case for restitution of conjugal rights and for restraining the husband from marrying a second time. But he was married before he could be called to the court. She carried on with the proceedings she had begun for restitution of conjugal rights.[16]

In the court's narrative, trouble arose between the husband and the wife some time after they were married, after she had "(borne) him a son." The "wife left the husband's house" and did not return. After "vain efforts at reconciliation", the husband married a second wife. It was for this "ulterior purpose" of preventing the husband marrying another time that the wife, "frustrated" in her "real purpose", brought the suit. This was not "in good faith at all." It was this that led the Sub-Judge to believe the case to have been "at the instigation of her father."[17]

---

13. Ganesh Prasad Ramprasad *v.* Damayanti, AIR 1946 Nag 60 (Niyogi, Bose and Sen JJ.).
14. Kishore Sahu *v.* Mrs. Snehprabha Sahu, AIR 1943 Nag 185 (Niyogi, Vivian Bose and Digby JJ.).
15. Rukibai *v.* Dr. Partabrai Godhumal, AIR 1938 Sind 233 (Davis JC and Weston J.).
16. *Ibid.*
17. *Ibid.*

The deep and sinister purpose of preventing the husband from marrying again lay revealed. There is a severe "aha, caught you!" in the judgment.

What was it about the wife's conduct that so raised the ire of the court? In the obligations imposed on a Hindu wife for the benefit of her husband, upon her marriage she should have become "one with the family of her husband." Yet, "(s)he has in her heart remained in the family of her father. She has sided with her father's house against her husband's house: she has refused all efforts at reconciliation and insulted and outraged his house by the charges of misconduct she has brought against him and his widowed sister-in-law." It was "clear that she left her husband's house without his permission; she did not . . . realise her position as a Hindu wife, and though it may well be that time and the spread of education have softened the harsh austerity of the simple rule that a Hindu wife must look on and revere her husband as a god, yet it is clearly her duty to honour and obey him. . ."[18]

It was clear to the court that though she had not been guilty of adultery, she had nevertheless deserted her husband's house. And she had sought an order for restitution of conjugal rights "not because in truth she wanted to live with her husband as one of two wives . . . but to punish him." The fact that she had "borne her husband a child" in itself not being "sufficient to outweigh her failure in other duties", and being "guilty of such unwifely conduct", she was not entitled to the order she sought. This failure to get an order, said the court in its wisdom, was not to prevent her "becoming reconciled with her husband, if good people should . . . intervene."[19]

The fact that a girl was only 9 years old when married, and that she lost her option of puberty since it was her father who gave her in marriage, is another dimension to nullity and divorce?[20] "Mere disparity in age" or the "tastes of the

18. *Ibid.*
19. *Ibid.* See also Kurma Pullamma *v.* Kurma Thatalingam, AIR 1945 Mad 44 (Kuppuswami Ayyar J.).
20. Fatima Bibi *v.* Mian Eusoof Sulaiman Ahmed, AIR 1937 Rang 361 (Roberts C.J. and Leach J.).

bride", not being relevant in Mohammedan law "must not be taken into account nor allowed to influence the decision."[21] Nor was it a relevant ground for divorce that a wife had begun to hate her husband.[22] The continuance of marriage at the cost of the woman stood reinforced.

The man petitions for divorce averring the woman's frigidity. The woman admits to coldness, frigidity and hysteria, brought on by the profusion of "his marital effusiveness" almost amounting to cruelty, and that her response had made her husband impotent in his relationship with her. The man does not contest this.[23]

The court finds the case "unusual." (The dissenting judge even finds it "unnatural.") There is a suspicion of collusion.[24] They are both professional actors and she had been a medical student for two years; that adds to the doubt about the facts in issue. The court believes the man, and, overcoming its reluctance to give him an order which will liberate the wife too, grants him a divorce. It asserts that there is much against the wife. For, while she swore she as a virgin, she refused to submit to a medical examination. She had not been wholly frank, they say, when she swore that there were no embraces before marriage; the man on the other hand, stated "that their courtship proceeded along normal lines (. . . from the standards of the West and of modern emancipated India)." Theirs was a mixed marriage and in the face of orthodoxy. Their profession is not noted for its sexual reticence. As a medical student she had made "a not too superficial study of the psychology of sex." And it is impossible to believe that "a woman who had told lies about her premarital relations with this man and who has this knowledge and background, and who says she has this

21. *Ibid.*

22. Umar-ul-Hafiz *v.* Talib Hussain, AIR 1945 Lah 56 (Abdur Rahman J.).

23. *Supra* n. 14.

24. It is a continuing paradox that, even after the introduction of divorce by mutual consent into the law, "collusion" between a husband and a wife who both desire divorce is a sin in the eyes of the law. A finding of collusion could deny them divorce.

psychological approach to marriage, would refuse to submit to a medical examination from motives of reticence."[25]

As if in penalty, she is directed to pay the cost of the proceedings because "the fault throughout has been hers, and because she has refused to assist the court by declining to submit to a medical examination; also because we do not think she has been frank."[26]

A post-script, quoting from the dissent: "The hysterical attitude is extremely strange," said the English judge, "in this country where one would expect a frank and natural approach to the physical fact of marriage."[27]

IV

Are there limits to judicial tolerance of a man venting his spleen on his wife? It appears the courts believed there was. "Small beatings" may not be legal cruelty,[28] and if a prisoner, coming from a poor class, had "chastised his wife moderately, but not sufficiently to do her serious damage", resulting in her death "probably no more would (have been) heard of the matter."[29] And while some in the lower rungs of the judicial hierarchy may deny a decree of judicial separation to a wife whose "hands were tied with a chain and her feet with a rope and she was kept hanging in a doorway", because "a few isolated acts of violence" were not enough to constitute legal cruelty, this view might well be overridden in appeal.[30] The higher, therefore wiser, court could yet reiterate that "(c)ruelty is, in its character, a cumulative charge", and it was the "repeated acts of violence" in that case which they termed legal cruelty.[31]

---

25. *Supra* n. 14.
26. *Ibid*. Compare it with the treatment of the woman in *supra* n. 9.
27. *Supra* n. 14.
28. Kamala Gangalamma *v.* Venkagarami Reddi, AIR 1950 Mad 385 (Panchapakesa Ayyar J.).
29. Emperor *v.* Koya Partab, AIR 1930 Bom 593 (2) (Beaumont CJ and Madgavkar J.).
30. Mary Brawne (Airs) *v.* A.N. Browne, AIR 1937 Oudh 52 (Nanavutty and Ziaul Hasan JJ.).
31. *Ibid*.

Subbia Goundan was charged with having voluntarily caused hurt to his 20 year old wife when he beat her, and with having injured her mother when she intervened, resulting in her death. The episode inspired the Sessions Judge to set out what he called "the right of the husband to beat his wife for impertinence and impudence."[32] The Sessions Judge was so "obsessed with his belief in the existence of such a right" that he launched into a criticism of the police for having included the charge of causing hurt to his (Subbia Goundan's) wife. While the Sessions Judge may be entitled to have his own views on the subject in a private capacity," the High Court said, "he was not justified in this manner from his seat on the Bench, and declaring in general and unqualified terms that a husband has the right of punishing his wife by beating her for impudence or impertinence." For, "no such general or unqualified right is nowadays recognised by law, and is not co-nominee one of the Exceptions in the . . . Penal Code. . . . We think it necessary to state in unmistakable terms that the learned Sessions Judge's declaration of the rights of husbands in this regard has no foundation, so that no one may rely upon that in future as a justification for wife-beating."[33]

It must have been these eminently thought-provoking debates which instigated learned tracts to be written on the subject. In an article on "How far it is lawful to chastise the wife under the Mahomedan law,"[34] the learned author, alluding to juristic works, decided cases and statutes deduces that after the Muslim Personal Law (Shariat) Act 26 of 1937 entered into force, "(t)he right of a Mahomedan husband to chastise is a matrimonial right and has been restored." Concerned and earnest, he concludes his article thus : "The right to beat the wife was abrogated by) statute law and by judicial decisions. Has it been restored (as we think it is) by Act 26 of 1937? Do the Mahomedans want to retain this right;

32. *In re* Subbia Goundan, AIR 1936 Mad 788 (Pandrang Row and Menon JJ.).

33. *Ibid.*

34. Jatindra Mohan Datta, "How far it is lawful to chastise the wife under the Mahomedan law", AIR 1940 Journal 25.

or abolish it by amending the legislation? These are very important questions and, we think, as lawyers we should take prominent part in moulding popular opinion in these respects."

The interest generated by the husband's right to beat his wife even inspired a book.[35] "The author has given a brief history of husband's right over his wife by referring to passages from the Holy Bible, the Holy Quran and the Manusmriti," runs a review. And adds that the book "affords interesting reading and can be read with profit by the Bench, the bar and laymen."[36]

The courts did draw a line somewhere. Nose-cutting was, indeed, too "vindictive and cruel."[37] Disfigurement as a factor in determining the gravity of the crime[38] and suspicions of 'unchastity'[39] recur in the proceedings. Disfigurement of a woman could lend a complexion of cruelty to an act, which mere beating could not always ensure. And allegations of adultery could excite ambivalence in the court.

There was the case for the prosecution which averred that the husband beat and ill-treated his wife, till he finally refused to maintain her.[40] She found employment as a maidservant in one Vassanmal's house. When she had been working there for a very few days, the husband met her on the road on her way to work, seized her by the hair, threw her to the ground, took out a dagger and carved up her face. There were 11 wounds, 10 on the face, forehead nose and near the eyes. The husband argued it was grave and sudden provocation. That she as an unchaste wife, he had met her by chance that day, lose self-control and struck her.

---

35. Anand S. Bhatnagar (approx. 1940), Husband's Right to Beat Wife, Allahabad Weekly Reporter Office. The book was 80 pages long.
36. "Review" at AIR 1940 Journal 51.
37. Emperor *v.* Bhano Bhojo, AIR 1944 Sind 186 (Davis CJ and O'Sullivan J.).
38. Kedarmal *v.* Crown, AIR 1950 Ajmer 13(1) (Ramabhadran JC): Emperor *v.* Ismail linear, AIR 1936 Bom 430 (Broomfield and Norman JJ.); Emperor *v.* Bhano Bhojo, *ibid.*
39. E.g., *supra* n. 37 and Emperor *v.* Ismail Umar, *ibid.*
40. *Supra* n. 37.

No credence was given to the husband's defence. The travails of the court talking around the aspersion of unchastity is telling. On the one hand, "we think that it must be made plain that aggrieved husbands, even those "they suspect their wives of unchastity, are not entitled to punish them in this cruel and vindictive manner", they said. Though, "we can concede that in this case the husband was angered, even distressed, by the circumstances in which his wife lived." "On the other hand, it is to be remembered that if a man turns his wife out of his house, she may perforce have to earn her living somewhere." On the other hand, yet again, she served in the house of Vassanmal, who kept a hotel. She was just 18, and "according to her own statement, visitors used to come to the house and she was called upon to bring them *pan* and others." "The surroundings were not desirable." Yet, again, "this appears . . . in no way to justify this cruel and barbaric assault upon this woman."[41]

There is a manner of limiting the apparent gravity of a crime that insinuates itself into the cases. The case goes before a Magistrate, and he could at most pass a sentence of 2 years rigorous imprisonment (RI); that is the extent of his power, and the charge gets reduced accordingly. Any appeal would be confined to applying this sentence as a maximum. In a sense, then, the crime is declared to deserve no more than two years RI. And, even after citing a "particularly brutal case" from 1892, where the husband had "tied his wife by her arms and legs to a bedstead and then cut off the whole of the soft parts of her nose, and a portion of her upper lip" for "the sole reason that the complainant would not live with the accused as his wife,"[42] the court drew back from making a heavy sentence into a probability. It expressed a preference for taking the case before the Magistrate as a matter of course, reference to the Court of Sessions being the exception.[43]

---

41. *Ibid.*
42. Queen Empress *v.* Abdul Rahiman (1892) 16 Bom 580 where the case was sent back to the Court of Sessions and a sentence of 8 years was passed.
43. Emperor *v.* Ismail Umar, *supra* n. 38.

V

This jurisprudence of the husband's right to beat his wife, and to be nominally punished when he steps beyond the tolerable, takes one into the region of maintenance.

The ground rules are: "(a) the husband must, *prima facie*, support his wife. This he can do by making her share his board and house."[44] It is only her comfort and safety which are relevant. Maintenance has no bearing on conjugal relations, except to the extent that such relations are rendered unsafe for the wife; impotence is, consequently, irrelevant in a demand for maintenance.[45] And a wife cannot insist that she should be treated as a member of the family with a right to live in the family home. For, "she was not entitled to be treated as a 'wife' but only to be maintained."[46] Also, an "unchaste woman is not entitled to anything but a 'bare' or 'starting' maintenance, and even that may be forfeited if she continues or persists in her unchaste life."[47] It is only wives who are entitled to maintenance-long years of living together does not invest the woman with the incidents of being a wife.[48]

Further, the "obligation of a husband to maintain his wife arises from the anxiety of the legislature to protect deserted wives from the bitter necessity of earning a living by trading on their sex. That obligation . . . ceases when it has been voluntarily assumed by some man other than the woman's husband. No woman can fairly claim a right to be kept by two men. But it is obviously not the law that a man may desert and neglect his wife and thus tempt her to unchastity and then resist her claim to be maintained by him on the ground that she is unchaste."[49]

---

44. Emperor *v.* Daulat Raibhan, AIR 1948 Nag 69 (Hidayatullah J.).
45. *Ibid.*
46. Arunachala Asari *v.* Anandayammal, AIR 1933 Mad 688 (Bum J.).
47. Bai Appibai *v.* Khimji Cooverji, AIR 1936 Bom 138 (B.J. Wadia J.).
48. A.T. Lakshmi Ambalam *v.* Andiammal, AIR 1938 Mad 66 (Newsam J.).
49. *Ibid.*

Habitual ill-treatment of the wife could draw varying responses at different rungs of the judicial hierarchy. So it was when a husband apparently developed intense dislike for his wife and "practically put her away" and brought another into the house as his mistress. "Time after time Hira has kicked and cuffed her. Time after time as a result of this ill-treatment the unfortunate woman has been compelled to run away (to) . . . the house of her father. Panchayats were convened on several occasions. The decree of the panchayat was that the wife should go back to her husband and try to make up with him . . . and . . . each time she became the object of her husband's abuse and inhuman oppression. On the last occasion . . . he kept her without food for a day or two and then turned her out."[50] This "abuse and inhuman oppression" of which the High Court spoke was treated with tolerance by the Magistrate, who said: "There are occasional outbursts of temper even in well organised families and it is not a matter of surprise or of unusual importance that there should have been such a treatment of the wife by the husband who are koris (by caste) and unfortunately not very civilised.. . ." A High Court judge, retorting perhaps ironically rather than accurately (as our experience with wife-beating tells us). said "I am not aware of any social rules prevailing in the Hindu system of society, at the present day and hour or in comparatively recent tames which allow or countenance the habitual ill-treatment of the wife by the husband nor am I aware of any custom in vogue which would compel the return of the wife to the husband in spite of his habitual ill-treatment. . . ."[51] This was of course belied by the decisions of the panchayats which the court spoke about. Perhaps the concern for the woman can be tracked to the opening paragraphs of the decision where it was said "No aspersion has been cast upon the character of Mt. Kaluiya. She has been a faithful wife and 'has kept unsullied the bed of her lord'. It has also not been alleged or proved that she has been guilty of such minor offences in the

50. Mt. Kaluiva *v.* Hira, AIR 1929 All 950 (Sen J.).
51. *Ibid.*

performance of her household duties which were in any way calculated to cause annoyance to or impair the comfort of her husband."[52]

Occasionally, a factor beyond chastity—a mere child of 14 who was a credible victim of rape by an absconder and yet stood excommunicated at a caste meeting[53]—may impress a court while deciding issues relevant to maintenance. Nevertheless, even where the charge of rape is not seriously doubted, it may surrender the sensitivities of the child-woman, and say: 'Even if the act of sexual intercourse was with the consent of the girl . . . it is a single isolated act", and then award her maintenance.[54]

Even more occasional is the 'naikin', married after entering into a prenuptial agreement to provide her with a separate house and motor car, ornaments of ancestral worth and to pay off her debts, being provided maintenance.[55] And, when her husband first denies the marriage, and later offers to take her back in his house, gets a court which says "it is true that the Hindu law enjoins implicit obedience on the wife. Her husband is to her as a 'god' or 'deity', and to be regarded as such. But the Hindu law (does not go) so far as to allow a husband to first abandon his wife, then to deny the validity of the marriage, then to neglect her and to refuse to have anything to do with her. . . ." and acknowledges her right to reside separately and be maintained.[56]

Between the early years of our study and 1950, something changed in the court's attitude to a wife who was relegated to being a first wife. In 1926, a court states, without challenging it, that "it has been held repeatedly that the marrying of a second wife would not justify a first wife to refuse to live with her husband". It then orders maintenance

---

52. *Ibid.* See also Mt. Tajbaro *v.* Ghulam Qadar, AIR 1933 Peshawar 101(1) (Middleton J.).
53. Yesubai *v.* Parasram Daji, AIR 1933 Bom 21 (Beaumont CJ and Nanavati J.).
55. *Supra* n. 47.
54. *Ibid.*
56. *Ibid.*
57. Pritam Singh *v.* Mt. Basant Kaur, AIR 1926 Lah 353 (Broadway J.).

because of continued ill-treatment.[57] Even in 1948, a court asserts that "the occasional lapse from virtue of a husband does not entitle the wife to ask for maintenance under Section 488, CrPC'. Scolding, it says, "a wife cannot refuse to go and live with the husband solely on the ground of his having a mistress" and cites authorities to bolster its stand.[58]

In 1946, the right of Hindu women to separate residence and to maintenance where the husband married again was recognised by statute.[59] Perhaps a court needed a law to assert that, where the husband married a second time, his offer of taking the wife back and treating her well could not be taken to be sincere. "Even if he takes her back", it said, "he will only make her an unpaid cook and maid for all work of himself and his second wife, an intolerable position and one to which no court should drive a married woman."[60] This is also an uncommon instance here the court considered the husband's having to maintain another wife as a relevant factor in computing maintenance.[61]

It was in 1948 that Justice Chagla expressly acknowledged that the movement of time creates anachronisms. And it was then that the passage of a law was used to break with habits of the past.[62] Fifty or hundred years ago concubinage may not have been looked upon with disfavour, he said, but that had changed by 1944, when the suit for maintenance in the case before him was instituted. It is not only physical cruelty, but also mental cruelty, that may justify a Hindu woman leaving her husband's house: and a transfer of affections to another woman could constitute such cruelty, he said. With that he introduced the law to the notion of "self-respect" of the wife. Generalising in time the

---

58. Rose Mary *v.* T.S. Arulswamy, AIR 1948 Mad 509 (Govinda Menon J.).
59. Hindu Married Women's Right to Separate Residence and Maintenance Act, 1946.
60. Senapathi Mudaliar *v.* Deivanai Ammal, AIR 1950 Mad 357 (Panchapakesa Ayyar J.).
61. *Ibid.*
62. Mallawa Shiddappa Ujjannavar *v.* Shiddappa Bhimappa Ujjannavar, AIR 1950 Bom 112 (Chagla CJ and Tendolkar J.).

content and import of the Hindu Married Woman's Right to Separate Residence and Maintenance Act 1946, he said, "This Act does not surely amend the Hindu law but it is also to a certain extent declaratory of Hindu law as it existed before the Act was passed."[63] Perhaps this decision represents a reinterpretation to erase judicial attitudes thus far exhibited, and to give a manner of retrospectivity to the treatment of women.

It was not beyond the law's reckoning that a daughter maintain her mother. But the daughter needs resources to meet a maintenance order. A Burmese Buddhist wife, as a dependent spouse, was as such entitled to one-third of her husband's salary; but a court would not recognise this entitlement as any definite share in his salary from which she could maintain her mother. It was there that the court definitely, and peremptorily, drew the line.[64]

VI

The visible woman with, and in the passive voice emerges while reckoning with her role as a lawful guardian. We also see her in a state of depleted autonomy. The father and the husband battle for the power of disposition or possession of the woman. It is in this struggle for control that a father is charged with procuring a minor girl (Section 366-A, IPC) when he tells his daughter to go away with him from a house where she was unhappy, and he will find her another husband for this was an inducement, and he had induced her as the law said he shouldn't. "It is true that those provisions were enacted to give effect to the International Convention for the Suppression of Traffic in Women and Children signed at Geneva in 1922", the court said. "When a married girl is unhappy with her husband and her father takes her from the husband's house and gives her as a wife to somebody else that can hardly be called trafficking in women. At the same time, having regard to the

63. *Ibid*. See also Lakshmi Animal *v.* Narayanaswami Naicker, AIR 1950 Mad 321 (Viswanatha Sastri J.).

64. Mating Kun *v.* Ma Kyaw Shin, AIR 1930 Rangoon 147 (2) (Das J.).

provisions of the section, I am of opinion that the act of the father would come within these provisions."[65]

It is in this delineation of power that a court holds that, under Hindu law, upon the marriage of a minor daughter, her father ceases to be her legal guardian and her husband takes over.[66] In silencing the woman, an 1889 decision gets cited, which says "It is immaterial whether the girl did or did not consent; she was kept against the will of those who were lawfully entitled to have charge of her and this keeping and the refusal to give up amounted to detention which was unlawful."[67] This sentiment is reinforced though the court did direct that the girl, being "old enough to form an intelligent judgment", be allowed her say before deciding about the husband "recover(ing) possession of his wife."[68]

It is in this contest between father and husband that the legally sanctified guardian finds himself indulged in his illegality. And a court may recognise the power of a civil court to decline custody to the husband and "permit her parents to retain her in their custody until she reaches maturity. But it by no means follows that, if such a husband seizes an opportunity that presents itself to him of taking his wife into his own custody, he commits a criminal offence." For, "(a) husband becomes the lawful guardian of his wife as soon as the marriage ceremony has been performed, and it is immaterial whether or not his wife has then attained puberty."[69]

The closing in on the woman effected through the guardian was again smuggled in when citing, in reiteration, a Punjab case where "it was held that providing shelter for a married woman was such an inducement as to amount to detention within the meaning of Section 498 (Penal Code)." There was no evidence of forcible detention, but that there

65. Ram Saran *v.* Emperor, AIR 1930 All 497 (Dalal J.).
66. Tulsidas Janglyadas *v.* Chetandas Domadas, AIR 1933 Nag 374 (Subedar AJC).
67. Abraham *v.* Mahtabo (1889) 16 Cal 487 quoted in *ibid.*
68. *Supra* n. 66.
69. Dhuma Manjhi *v.* Emperor, AIR 1943 Pat 109 (Meredith and Shearer JJ.).

was persuasion was enough to indict the man in whose house the woman"was found."[70]

The irrelevance of the woman's reason, emotion, need, determination and choice was thus combined with the threat of punishment held out to any who might respond to her unhappiness or suffering, or who represented her expression of will and choice.

VII

When a girl, less than 15 years old, commits suicide; there is information that she had been "systematically ill-treated, beaten, abused and prevented from going to her parents" by her mother-in-law and her husband; police investigation leads to the mother-in-law being charged, and the court absolves her because her son had not been jointly charged, it adds a poignancy to the plight of the child-bride.[71] Even as the court denied a pride of place to the question of custody or legal custody" to prosecute under the Bengal Children's Act, 1922, it yet said that the evidence shoved that the "deceased girl was living with her husband in the husband's house, and . . . the mother-in-law also lived there", but that was not enough to establish that the mother-in-law had "custody, charge or care of the deceased girl" in fact.[72] So we see the infiltration of the fiction of the legal guardian into the decision, even as the court denied its relevance.

A word in passing this apparent reluctance to find a woman culpable should not be mistaken to be willingness of the court generally to protect women from punishment. We do encounter at least two instance of the death penalty being passed on 'women for stealing ornaments off 12 year old children and killing them. The youth of the convicted

---

70. Banarsi Raut *v.* Emperor, AIR 1938 Pat 432 (Agarwala J.).
71. Bhagwati Devi *v.* Emperor, AIR 1938 Cal 638 (Bartley and Khundkar JJ.).
72. *Ibid.* Section 40 of the Bengal Children's Act, 1922 provided punishment for who had custody, charge or care of a child or young person if they ill-treated, neglected, abandoned . . . the child or young person. . .

women—20 and 22—and that they had, in each case, delivered a child while in jail, were not considered extenuating circumstances.[73] The court did suggest that the Local Government may take these factors into account in answer to a plea for clemency, but they should not, it considered, weigh with the court.[74]

Whatever the law, it is manifest in decisions in cases of infanticide that the court found itself moved to finding a way of lessening the charge from murder. This they did when they held that a woman who had jumped into a well with her child—she survived and the child died—had caused the death of the child by "negligent omission", "the omission to put the child down before jumping into the well." She was given a sentence of 6 months' simple imprisonment. In the alternative, where they found themselves bound by the law to affirm a sentence of transportation for life, the judgment would conclude with a persuasive recommendation to the Local Government for a much shorter sentence.[76]

VIII

Returning to the theme of the guardian, there is the instance of this politically active 17 year old who, when part of a procession taken out without permission of the District Magistrate, was arrested with seven others under the Defence of India Rules, 1939. While three of her compatriots apologised and were let off, she was among those sentenced,

73. *In re* Thalappil Thithachumma, AIR 1941 Mad 27 (Bum and Mockett JJ.) and Mt. Jamunia Partap Lohar *v.* Emperor, AIR 1936 Nag 200 (Grille and Gruer JJ.).
74. *Ibid.*
75. Supadi Lukadu *v.* Emperor, AIR 1925 Bom 310 (Pratt and Crump JJ.). See also Mt. Hasson Pari *v.* Emperor, AIR 1941 Peshawar 22 (Almond JC and Soofi J.).
76. Ghulam Jannat *v.* Emperor, AIR 1926 Lah 271 (Shadi Lal CJ and Zafar Ali J.) where they recommended three years RI and Mt. Alan, Bibi *v.* Emperor, AIR 1932 Lah 297 (Harrison and Dalip Singh JJ.) where the recommended sentence was one year RI.

to one year's RI and a fine of Rs. 100. While one of her convicted friends appealed. she did not.[77]

Her father did. And he was allowed to. It gave the Chief Justice the opportunity to deliver a peroration on the nature of a "political offence" and its disruptive consequences, and to comment. "No doubt, the fine will probably have to be paid by the parent, but after all parents may reasonably be expected to restrain the activities of their children when those activities conflict with the law. The effect of imposing a fine is to give the parent the option of keeping the child out of jail by a moderate payment." With that and a comment that he wouldn't have imposed a sentence of more than 4 months' RI, the sentence of imprisonment was reduced to the period already undergone, which was 6 months.[78]

The judgment makes no pretense of having let the girl speak at any time in these appeal proceedings. Her father was permitted to appropriate, and demolish, her politics. She was the only girl who had gone to conviction and sentence, and the opportunity that her father gave to the court to lecture, and release, her—one that she refused to provide by not appealing—inhabits the silent spaces in this judgment.

It may be mentioned here that the mother, "not answer(ing) the description of either the father or the guardian", has no role in giving consent to a marriage under the Special Marriage Act, 1872.[79]

The reasonableness of the outrageous was written into K's case. When K came of age, her mother took her back home from her husband's house. Her husband approached the court asking that she be "restored to his lawful custody" mother responded that the girl was just 13 and "not in a fit condition for consummation. Apart from her young age, she is also in poor health and undergoing medical treatment." She therefore pleaded "in the interests of the minor that

77. Emperor *v.* Kamal Dattatraya Sohoni, AIR 1943 Bom 304 (Beaumont CJ and Weston J.).

78. *Ibid.*

79. *Supra* n. 13.

immediate custody of her daughter should not be directed to be given" to the husband.[80]

For the court, the first concern was whether the remedy to recover custody of his minor wife "illegally detained by others" existed in criminal law. The answer was, it did. Then, it was a question of whether the husband became the lawful guardian "and therefore entitled to her custody." In one word, "undoubtedly." In fact, "(e)ven if the girl desires to stay with her mother . . . that would not confer a right on the (mother) to detain her."[81]

Yet, K was a minor and "this court should have, as the paramount consideration, her interest and welfare", and the mother's "fear that the (husband) requires the custody of her daughter in order that the consummation of the marriage should take place" not being unfounded, a suggestion made by the husband that "gladdened" the court, was adopted. "If this Hon'ble Court is of opinion that the consummation may be postponed," he had said, "the minor may be ordered to be kept in the custody of some public institution such as Sevasadan and not with the (mother) for a reasonable period and I am prepared to meet the expenses." Having regard to this attitude of the husband which "cannot be said to be unreasonable", K's mother was directed "to surrender her minor daughter to the (husband) forthwith on condition that (he) should arrange to have . . . K . . . kept in the custody of some public institution for the period of one year and incur the necessary expenses for the purpose."[82]

A police constable lodges a complaint of adultery against four persons who he alleges are "carrying on an intrigue with his wife." The Magistrate issues a warrant permitting a search to be undertaken for a person wrongfully confined.[83] Upon search, the wife is arrested. With nothing to

---

80. P. Venkataramaniah Chetty *v.* Pappamah, AIR 1948 Mad 103 (Rajamannar J.). See also Om Radhe *v.* Emperor, AIR 1939 Sind 152 (Lobo and Weston JJ.).

81. *Ibid.*

82. *Ibid.*

83. Section 100 of the Criminal Procedure Code 1898: Section 97 of the Criminal Procedure Code 1973.

indicate that the wife was confined under circumstances which would be an offence, the Magistrate yet proceeds to make an order "consigning her to a certain ashram in Calcutta."[84] The High Court. on appeal, records that "(t)he information before the Magistrate was that the petitioner was living in her mother's house, and there was not even a suggestion that she was being detained by her mother against her will", "prefacing her release from irregular imprisonment" with the legal sentiment that "(s)he was as much entitled to her liberty as anybody else", reinforcing the importance of access to appeal.[85]

While still on the use of institutions, we may dwell a while on the disadvantage of belonging to a sex which has relatively few who transgress the law. Adolescent girls couldn't be sent to Borstal School since it was only for boys. Without further inquiry, it was presumed that "some arrangement is . . . made in the women's jail at Velicre for segregating adolescent offenders from the hardened adult ones." And the weight shifted from the court's shoulders: "In any event, that is a matter for the government to arrange and the court can only impose such sentences as it thinks proper and leave the government to make such arrangements as are possible for the protection of adolescents."[86] The economics of running institutions governing the existence and scale of schools, homes and jails, and with courts not insisting that a distinction be maintained, it is surely a prescription for the steady trickle of girls into adult penal institutions.

IX

Possession and control of the woman by the man to whom she belongs has nurtured, in law, notions of adultery, seduction and enticement. Fathers seeking to retrieve their

84. Thankamani Debi *v.* Nepal Chandra Bhattacharyya, AIR 1938 Cal 704 (Bartley and Henderson JJ.).
85. See also Raghubar Dayal *v.* Emperor, AIR 1938 Oudh 81 (Ziaul Hasan J.).
86. Public Prosecutor *v.* Rajam Ammal, AIR 1942 Mad 674 (Horwill J.).

daughters from the men they—the daughters—choose to live with resort to charging the other man with kidnapping, abducting or inducing the daughters to compel them into marriage. The popularity of this provision has had the court remark that it is "unfortunately a section which comes before the court possibly more often than any other particular section in the (Penal) Code, except those of riot and hurt."[87]

The offence of enticing away a married woman[88] would "depriv(e) the husband of his proper control over his wife for the purpose of illicit intercourse." Where a woman had been "carrying on an illicit intrigue" with a man other than her husband, and it "did not require a great deal of persuasion" to "induce (her) to leave her home", man would still be subjected to the punitive regime. For "providing a shelter for her was an inducement to her to withhold herself from her husband", making the man guilty in law.[89]

The tort of seduction raises questions about what is lost when seduction happens. A suit for seduction would be to recover damages from the offending outsider. Where the daughter is seduced, it is the father who has a right of action against the offending man; and with the father's death, the suit would not survive for the family to prosecute.[90] It is the legal obligation of a father to maintain his daughter and to perform her marriage. "Any seduction of an unmarried daughter not only impairs the honour and reputation of the family but increases the pecuniary burden owing to the difficulty of getting her married thereafter."[91] Yet, it ought not to be missed that the daughter herself can have no remedy against a seducer, since the courts do recognise that seduction takes place "by her own consent."[92]

---

87. Baijnath *v.* Emperor, AIR 1932 All 409 (Boys and Young JJ.).
88. Section 498, Indian Penal Code 1860.
89. Mohammad Aslam Khan *v.* Emperor, AIR 1937 Lab 617 (Abdul Rashid J.).
90. Baboo *v.* Mt. Subanshi, AIR 1942 Nag 99 (Stone CJ and Vivian Bose J.).
91. *Ibid.*
92. *Ibid.*

"However deeply the feelings of the parent may be affected by the wicked act of the seducer, the law gives no redress, unless the daughter is also a servant", the loss of service being the material factor.[93] But, where the husband is the offended individual, the case "stands on a different footing from that of a servant or daughter because there is a contract of marriage between the husband and the wife."[94] "It is not the mere depriving of a husband for a day or two which gives rise to this action it is the fact that the defendant has acted in a way towards the wife of the plaintiff which is illegal, and which he is not entitled to do."[95]

The man's right to possession and control over the woman's sexual life is reinforced when it is said that to "sustain a conviction for adultery, it must be established inter alia that sexual intercourse was committed without the consent or connivance of the husband."[96]

The logic of leniency to a woman who had been deserted by her husband and who had then lived with another, was advocated by the court, quoting a 1911 decision[97] for support. The earlier decision read: "Some people think that they must treat men and women on the same footing. But this court has not taken, and I hope will never take, that view. I trust that in dealing with these cases it will be ever remembered that the woman is the weaker vessel; that her habits of thought and feminine weaknesses are different from those of the man; and that what may perhaps be excusable in the case of the woman would not be excusable in the case of men. Where you find that the woman has been guilty of adultery and that her adultery has resulted from her husband's conduct towards her, this court does and I hope always will make allowances in treating her error with leniency."[98]

---

93. Tika Ram *v.* Sobha Ram, AIR 1935 All 855 (Ganga Nath J.).
94. Sobha Ram *v.* Tika Ram, AIR 1936 All 454 (Sulaiman CJ and Bennet J.).
95. *Ibid.*
96. Waroo *v.* Emperor, AIR 1948 Sind 40 (O'Sullivan J.).
97. Pretty *v.* Pretty (1911), p. 83.
98. *Ibid.* quoted in Gladys Bourke *v.* Richard Edmund Bourke, AIR 1932 Sind 18 (Milne J.) which was a case under the Divorce Act 1869.

The woman displays "sheer contempt for the husband"; the husband took no action for eight months after she turned a Mahomedan and had lived for months as the wife of another man. Then the court convicted the other man, even if it did reduce the sentence to the period already undergone.[99] In such a case as this, voluntariness, rejection and choice stood negatived for the woman, while the nature of property rights over the woman and the criminality of anyone else taking over possession was reasserted. Her autonomy was, of course, not even a possibility.

A man ought to be a man. So, when a man was "not master in his house", where his wife was "supreme" and she seemed "to be a woman of not only a strong will but of strong muscles too", her "preferential fondness" for another man did not lead to conviction of the other man. Emphasising control rather than possession, it was said: "The legislature seems to require that the enticement of the wife must be from the control of the husband before the enticer can be convicted under Section 498 Penal Code. If however there is no such control at all of the husband over the wife then . . .", surely, there can be no punishment.[100]

How is a man to value his loss when his wife leaves him for another? The Divorce Act 1869 will have the other man, or men, pay damages to the husband.[101] The extent of the loss has however to be assessed by the court.

So it is to be remembered that "the object of the damage is not punitive"[102] but "compensatory."[103] The means of the co-respondent (as the other man becomes, in the petition for divorce on the ground of the wife's adultery) have nothing to do with the question of the quantum of

---

99. Gahra *v.* Emperor, AIR 1926 Lah 176 (Abdul Raoof J.).

100. Gul Mahomed *v.* Emperor, AIR 1934 Sind 10 (Dadiba C. Mehta AJC).

101. Section 34, Divorce Act, 1869: "Husband may claim damages from adulterer. . ."

102. Arthur John Mackinley *v.* M.D. Mackinley, AIR 1932 Oudh 182 (Kisch J.).

103. Niranjan Das Mohan (Dr.) *v.* Mrs. Ena Mohan w/o Dr. Niranjan Das Mohan, AIR 1943 Cal 146 (Nasim Ali and Rau JJ.).

damages."[104] "It is not the intention that a man should make a profit out of the dishonour of his wife. The only question is what the (husband) has lost in his wife."[105]

It follows that a judge should, therefore, consider whether, in the past, his wife was "a good wife and took good care of his house and children." For, "if she were a worthless wife, always out of the house and not attending to her duties", the husband may not be entitled to any damages at all.[106] It once was found to have been that "the wife was a good wife to him", they lived happily together for 10-11 years when the co-respondent formed an "improper acquaintance with the wife; he took her away; the husband got the wife back again and gave her another chance for some two or three months, and then the co-respondent abducted the wife a second time, and has been living with her ever since." And the will-less wife was effectively effaced in this description of a tussle between man and man.

Incidentally, the "proper sum" to compensate for the loss of the wife was, here, Rs. 300.[107]

It could be different where the husband's own character and conduct are responsible for his wife leaving him, and turning to the co-respondent for support. Particularly when she knew that apart from the precarious assistance her parents could give her, she had no means to support herself and her child. The court would still give him damages. And the husband may claim Rs. 25,000, and the court may grant a "nominal sum" of Rs. 500.[108]

It could differ again where he was a good husband, treated his wife well, his home was broken up, his feelings lacerated, and he also had to suffer "the slur of losing his

---

104. Charles Wakehearst Peyton *v.* Mrs Ada Peyton, AIR 1937 Lah 417 (Coldstream, Skemp and Abdul Rashid JJ.).

105. Freer *v.* Johnson, AIR 1924 Mad 446. See also Gopi *v.* Mt. Hiriya, AIR 1935 Nag 49 (Grille JC and Niyogi and Staples JJ.).

106. Premchand Hira *v.* Bai Galal, AIR 1927 Bom 594 (Marten CJ and Crump and Baker 13).

107. *Ibid.*

108. *Supra* n. 102.

wife." The court may then find Rs. 3000 not excessive.[109] Or, in the occasional case, the court may distribute justice by reckoning the value of the wife to the husband at Rs. 2000, and get the co-respondent to pay the wife Rs. 1000 when he leaves her to marry another woman.[110]

What questions would a court ask in measuring damages? It may be: "(1) How has the husband demeaned himself? (2) Did he and his wife live happily together? Because if they lived unhappily his loss in his wife is not so great. (3) The position of the defendant" (co-respondent).[111] Or a court may be concerned with the actual value of the wife to the husband, (2) the proper compensation for the injury to his feelings, the blow to his marital honour and the serious hurt to his matrimonial and family life."[112]

Emerging from amidst the concern to compensate the husband for loss of his wife may be a recognition of the pecuniary contribution of a woman to her home-reaching beyond her standard description as cook and governess. Where the wife had inherited "half a lakh of rupees and some house property from her father", and she was "in particular . . . look(ing) after the education of the children", her money worth to the husband could be capitalised at Rs. 2400.[113] As for the husband's feelings, "though they must have been considerably blunted" by the conduct of adultery on various occasions with various persons,"their intrigues must have destroyed any remaining chances of a reconciliation" and "have caused further injury to his feelings, however much they may have been blunted already." Where there was more than one co-respondent, as it happened here, the liability for damages may be shared out among them.[114]

The court-fee conundrum which encountered the husband when he went to court for restitution of conjugal

---

109. Sydney Arthur Hamilton *v.* Alice Maude Hamilton, AIR 1933 Sind 134 (Ferrers JC and Aston and Mehta AJCs).

110. *Supra* n. 104.

111. D'Cruz *v.* Mrs. D'Cruz, AIR 1927 Oudh 34 (Kendall J.).

112. *Supra* n. 103.

113. *Ibid.*

114. *Ibid.*

rights, and seeking an "injunction restraining the parents and other relations of the wife from obstructing the recovery of the wife by the husband", is a tale told by two earnest, eminent and learned judges. The value of the wife to the husband was at the nucleus of the debate. If the husband averred that he valued her at over Rs. 5000, he could have the attention of the High Court as a court of appeal; he placed her value, therefore, at Rs. 5001. But the Stamp Reporter and the Registrar found that, valued at Rs. 5001, the husband would have to pay an *ad valorem* scale of stamp duty since he desired not merely to retrieve his wife, but also to prevent others from obstructing his recovery. That was more than the husband desired to invest in getting his way with, and about, his wife.[115]

There was earlier a provision in the Court-fees Act, 1870 which read:

> "Plaint or memorandum of appeal in a suit for possession of a wife Rs. 5" and this had been repealed. Also, the provision which applied to situations where the approximate money value of the "subject-matter in dispute" was not possible to estimate would not be relevant, because "there are ordinarily several criteria available, to enable the plaintiff to arrive at an approximate valuation, e.g., dower, the amount which the husband may have to spend on the maintenance of his wife elsewhere than in his own house or the extra cost of domestic assistance for the performance of household work." And, in a further statement of the pragmatism of valuation, it was said: "This decision (holding that court-fees would have to be paid on an *ad valorem* scale) will not make it difficult for a poor person to institute suits for declaration that he is entitled to exercise conjugal rights and to obtain an injunction for he can put any value he likes on his wife."[116]

115. Gajendra Nath Saha Chowdhury *v.* Sulochana Chaudhurani, AIR 1935 Cal 338 (Mitter and Edglee JJ.).

116. *Ibid.*

Such were the considerations which were to dictate the worth of a wife.

XI

The premium on chastity brought slander and defamation into both civil and criminal jurisdictions. There is, after all, "no reason why a slanderer of women should not be made liable both civilly and criminally, just as, say, the driver of a motor car who runs over a woman by his rashness and negligence."[117]

It was "undoubtedly defamatory" to publish an article which indicates that "an unmarried girl of the Brahmin community who is well connected, had not preserved her virgin purity. One can hardly imagine a grosser kind of defamation."[118] And an amount of Rs. 1500 may be ordered as damages.[119]

Slandering a woman by stating that her husband is impotent and that the child born to her was by another man was definitely defamation. "To impute unchastity to a married woman is regarded so seriously in England that it is actionable *per se* in civil cases for slander. I have yet to learn that the people of India, taken as a whole, value the chastity of their women any less highly. This is especially so when, as here, an imputation of this kind is taken so seriously that outcasting promptly follows any suspicion of infidelity. It would be unfortunate for courts to apply any lesser standard in India, except of course among particular tribes or castes.. . ."[120]

Defamatory remarks made in the heat of the moment, when quarrelling, would not invite the court to interfere. For, "if all such remarks could invariably form the subject of a

117. Hirabai Jehangir Mistry *v.* Dinshaw Edulji Karkaria, AIR 1927 Bom 22 (Marten CJ and Kemp J.).

118. Edara Venkayya Pantulu *v.* Kalipattapu Chitti Surya Prakasamma, AIR 1940 Mad 879 (Pandrang Rao and Abdur Rahman JJ.).

119. *Ibid.*

120. Sukhdayal *v.* Mt. Saraswati, AIR 1937 Nag 122 (Vivian Bose J.).

civil suit, the courts would be swamped with trivial litigation. How often in India in criminal cases one reads the evidence,' He then began to abuse me by my female relations."[121]

A criminal complaint of defamation may be made by a person aggrieved. "While (this) excludes complaints by busybodies and mischief-makers, it does not say that the complaint can only be made by the person defamed."[122] The question therefore was "whether the husband is aggrieved when imputations are made upon the chastity of his wife." And it was decided that "(i)n view of the social customs prevailing amongst the community to which the parties belong, there can be no question that the husband would suffer very serious social disadvantages on account of these imputations." When it had been earlier held that a brother is an aggrieved person when imputations were made against the chastity of a widowed sister living with him,[123] "(t)he case of the husband is clearly stronger."[124]

Yet, a question may arise, as it did, whether a married woman could recover damages from a slanderer without proof of special damage. The conflict within the law grew out of the general rule that the law to be administered in India would be English law "as nearly as the circumstances of the place, and of the inhabitants, should admit." English law had it that proof of special damage was not needed where the slanderous words imputed a criminal offence. However, in England unchastity was not a criminal offence; in India it was. But in India the woman in an adulterous relationship was protected from conviction and punishment as an abettor, even as the offence of adultery as defined in criminal law imputed that she was a party to a criminal offence. Applying the English rule would have meant that the man who was alleged to be committing adultery could sue, while the slandered woman would have to prove special damage before

121. *Supra* n. 117.

122. Dwijendra Nat. 1, Talukdar *v.* Makhon Lal Pramanik, AIR 1943 Cal 564 (Henderson J.).

123. Thakur Das *v.* Adhar Chandra, 8 Cal WN 515 referred to in *ibid.*

124. *Supra* n. 122.

she could recover damages. The English law was therefore modified for Indian conditions to retain the position of the husband as sinned against by the adulterer even while allowing the wife to recover damages for being called unchaste and adulterous. For the court specified: ". . . our decision does not affect those cases of the slander of women, where the crime of adultery with a married woman is not involved."[125]

In another context, the "(d)eliberate attribution of immorality falsely to a wife will certainly fall under the definition of legal cruelty", entitling a woman to live separately from her husband and to claim maintenance.[126]

It was the perils of defamation law which Mt. G encountered. Mt. G's husband was detained in the police station while a charge of theft was being investigated against him. One day, Mt. G said, the SI of Police summoned her at night to the police station, questioned her about the stolen property and, on her denial of any knowledge, raped her. She asked that an investigation be made and the SI punished. The DSP ordered an enquiry and, "as he considered that the enquiry completely exonerated the SI of the charges", the SI preferred a complaint against Mt. G. The charge was that she had falsely charged the SI with having committed an offence intending that such charge cause him injury.[127]

The Sessions Judge speculated in his judgment—an 'on-the-one-hand . . .' manner of speculation-and acquitted her on a technical ground, that Mt. G had not intended to set the criminal law in motion—an improbable premise that the High Court roundly rejected. Yet the High Court too, in a stage aside, ranged over an array of reasons for discrediting her complaint. Perhaps she did it to hamper the investigation. Or may be it was revenge for implicating her husband in the crime. The court ended up with acquitting her, but not before it acknowledged "There are . . . circumstances in the course

125. *Supra* n. 117.

126. *Supra* n. 28.

127. Local Government *v.* Mt. Guji, AIR 1935 Nag 69 (Grille JC and Pollock AJC). See Section 211, Indian Penal Code, 1860.

of his investigation, which call for explanation, and that explanation has not been afforded. While . . . there was no evidence on the record to lead to the conclusion that G was raped as she alleges and that there is a great probability that her report was grossly exaggerated . . . (u)ndoubtedly some incidents took place that night which the SI was desirous of concealing. The threat, and harassment, of criminal proceedings, and the disincentive it would be for women who were raped, went without comment.[128]

XII

A woman, and of a low caste, protesting and setting the criminal law in motion, and the complaint coming to trial and punishment, is rare enough to cause comment. Even if it was reversed in appeal by a different perspective on caste. What the woman alleged was assault with intent to dishonour her, and no grave and sudden provocation to explain away the dishonour.[129]

The High Court perceived the facts, thus, the accused was "an orthodox Hindu . . . Brahmin" who "had taken his usual bath and was sitting on a stone in the midst of a stream offering his prayers. While he was performing his sandhyawandan and meditating on the object of his worship and reciting some prayer . . . a low caste woman passed through the stream at such close distance from that place that the surface of the water got naturally disturbed and some particles of water fell on his body. The contact of such water particles causes pollution and necessitates the taking of a fresh bath before the prayer can be completed. . . . Such interference or break in one's prayer ought to upset not merely a hasty or hot-tempered person, but even any person of ordinary sense and calmness. . . . There was besides an exchange of abuse and this provoked the accused a great deal. The trying Magistrates have after rejecting whatever

128. *Ibid*. See also Swee Ing *v*. Koon Han, AIR 1935 Rangoon 163 (Mackney J.).

129. Sheodia *v*. Mt. Jumni, AIR 1927 Nag 47 (Kinkhede AJC).

exaggeration there was in the story told by the complainant, definitely found that the accused acted under provocation when he caught hold of (her) hand."[130]

The District Magistrate thought otherwise, but the High Court offered this explanation: "(He) being of a different religion could not be expected to know much about the feelings and religious susceptibilities of an orthodox Hindu Brahmin. . . ."[131]

"I am entitled to presume," the judge said, "that the condition of the mind of the accused must necessarily have been such as gave him adequate cause to act in the manner he did, with due regard to decency and to the fact that the person who offended and disturbed him in his religious pursuits was after all a woman." He must have acted as he did to "(curb at once the insolent behaviour and the abusive retort . . . and he must have felt . . . that the best way to curb or check her was to catch hold of her hand to attain that object and to make her feel that he could not be so trifled with by her." In fact, "if the person insulting him had been a male, I fancy, he might have even beaten him or given him a sound thrashing."[132]

It was thus that honour gave place to presumed piety. And the sinned against was dubbed the sinner.

XIII

Death for dishonour and disobedience, infidelity and impertinence, was in the law's routine.[133] This was a time

---

130. *Ibid.*

131. *Ibid.*

132. *Ibid.*

133. A note before launching into the next part I am quite definitely opposed to the death penalty. I do not believe killing should be a state response to crime. I believe the continuance of the death penalty is one of the reasons that helps justify encounter killings, shoot-at-sight actions and custodial violence and death—since killing by the state is given legitimacy by retaining the penalty of death. I do not believe the death penalty is necessary for deterring the criminal—the criminal is already in the custody of the state. I do not

when, on conviction for murder, the imposition of the sentence of death was the norm, and reducing the penalty to less than death—usually transportation for life—required special reasons to be detailed in the judgment. This, it appears, was also a time when (was) exceedingly common" and allegations of adultery were often enough to convince a court to commute.

A court may have said, "we do not think that mere suspicion of a wife's conduct is any extenuation of a deliberate murder" especially where "the evidence shows the wife to have been a perfectly well behaved woman, whom the appellant treated very ill."[134] And the court may therefore have even enhanced a sentence to death because it would not "wish to offer any encouragement to the idea that men can butcher their wives and escape hanging on the plea that they suspected them of misconduct."[135]

Also, the "mere fact that a woman has been unfaithful to her husband is not in itself . . . sufficient ground for substitution of the lesser sentence where there was deliberate premeditation."[136]

In another time and age, it might impose the death penauy where it concluded that "the accused went to the deceased (wife's) house with the object of causing her

---

believe it furthers general deterrence, particularly where there is such scant information on the less sensational cases. Also, I do not believe one person should be killed to set an example to others. It is retributive in its intent and effect, and retribution can be no function of the state. I believe it is a penalty heavily weighted against the poor and the socially disadvantaged. And, to state one more of the many, many reasons that exist, I do not believe that judicial process, whose most commendable attribute is its non-violence should be engaged in the premeditated killing of any person.

It was not the sentence itself which drew my attention to these cases; it was the reasoning which the court found for justifying the death sentence, or in commuting the sentence to transportation for life, or less.

134. Dasan *v.* Emperor, AIR 1929 Mad 495 (Waller and Pandalai JJ.).

135. *Ibid.*

136. *Ibid.*

injury in case she did not follow him and accede to his wishes."[137]

Combining allegations of impudence with adultery, the husband may have sought understanding from the court, but found rebuke instead. Visiting her father's house without the husband's permission was no excuse for killing her, and the "penalty of death is the only possible one in the circumstances."[138]

A wedding in the village. Women assembled in the courtyard, singing. The husband calls his wife away as, he says, their children are crying. She says she will return in a while. He repeats his request three times, and receives the same reply. An hour later, when he calls her, she says she will go after the sweetmeats are distributed. Asked again, she says, "go and I will come home." Excited, he strikes her with a toka. She ducks. The blow falls on the 18 year old woman sitting beside her. Applying the doctrine of "transferred malice", he has committed the crime of murder. But, says the court, it is the lesser penalty that should be imposed, for "(h)e did not strike the blow with the intention of killing his wife and had been provoked by her repeated refusal to go home and take care of the children."[139]

Carefully recorded words of the husband may tell the court "how the woman was recalcitrant in the presence of the panchayat and answered them back by saying that, whether she had any intrigue with Pragi or not, when she was charged she would carry on an intrigue from that moment." The "words of wisdom" of the panch telling her that "married life should not be broken and her husband's offer the next morning that "he was prepared to pay fine and overlook any offence committed in the past" and that they move out of the village, appears to have prompted a sharp retort from her; which, in effect, was to let her be.

137. Fazal Karim *v.* Emperor, AIR 1936 Lah 580 (Young CJ and Monroe J.).

138. *In re* Manicka Nagendra Bagavathar, AIR 1950 Mad 484 (Govinda Menon and Basheer Ahmed Sayeed JJ.).

139. Rahman *v.* Emperor, AIR 1932 Lah 14 (Addison and Abdul Qadir JJ.).

"(A) shameless answer", said the court, "sufficient to give fresh provocation which would help condone the severity of the crime" of murdering her. "After the panchayat the husband was in hopes that his forgiving temper may win over his wife and the answer which he received of a determination to leave him and to disgrace him must have come upon him with sudden force." So it was that the wife's conduct made it no longer a crime of murder, but one of culpable homicide not amounting to murder, to be punished with a 7 year term of imprisonment.[140]

Perhaps the court did not see the provocation represented in forgiveness where there was no fault?

The infidelity of the wife, particularly where she refused to sever the relationship that existed outside her marriage, may make the court reduce the sentence from death to transportation for life.[141] And where the murdered person is the other man, the court may even be moved to suggest to the Local Government to consider reducing the sentence substantially. "There is no doubt that the provocation was grave," the court said, "and that although technically the offence comes under Section 302 the provocation was so extreme that it is not surprising that Jagar Jat killed Moman Jat."[142]

This indulgence was not extended to "a Baluchi who suspects that so ignominious an encroachment has been made upon his conjugal privileges. . ." and resorts, not to the law, but to murder. "There is a deliberate resolution to set law at defiance", the court observed, and denied tolerance, for, "we have already, and as long ago as 1913,[143] laid down the rule that the Baluchi custom of killing for unchastity cannot be taken into consideration in the mitigation of sentence."[144]

---

140. Suba *v.* Emperor, AIR 1928 Lah 344 (Broadway and Tek Chand JJ.).
141. Gurdin *v.* Emperor, AIR 1925 Oudh 288 (Dalal JC).
142. Ibrahim *v.* Emperor, AIR 1928 Lab 544 (Shadi Lal CJ and Bhide J.).
143. Jagar Beg Jat *v.* Emperor, AIR 1937 Lab 692 (Young CJ and Monroe J.).
144. Emperor *v.* Rahim Khan 18 Cri LJ 501.

Yet while it "is well established law that if a husband discovers his wife in the act of adultery and thereupon kills her he is guilty of manslaughter only and not of murder. But that rule has no application where the relationship between the parties is not that of husband and wife."[145] Not even if it is a person he is engaged to marry.[146]

It is the status of a woman as a wife, then, that particularly attracts the notion of person as property.

The means and the motive for murder in the home appear distinct for women and men. Men were found to have drowned,[147] strangled[148] or truncheoned[149] their wives. Women were generally brought in on charges of poisoning their husbands. Dhatura, the stuff of which the fiction of Agatha Christie was made, was the poison most commonly used. Men were provoked by suspicions of infidelity and by impertinence. Women were found to have been led to murder after "a severe beating" and threats that she would be killed;[150] "to recapture her husband's failing attentions" where she mistook the poison for a love potion;[151] or "to be free to continue her relations with her paramour."[152] The court's response ranged from acquittal,[153] to reduction of charge from murder to causing hurt by means of poison and a consequent reduction of sentence to 6 months' imprisonment,[154] to the death penalty, where the court did not believe she did not

145. Kaim Dilmurad *v.* Emperor, AIR 1935 Sind 44 (Ferrers JC and Dadiba C. Mehta AJC).
146. Emperor *v.* Dinabandhu Ooriya, AIR 1930 Cal 199 (Muter and S.K. Ghose JJ.).
147. *Ibid.* quoting Rex *v.* Palmer (1913) 2KB 29.
148. Ghulam Mohammad *v.* Emperor, AIR 1934 Lah 675 (2) (Agha Haidar J.).
149. Khanun *v.* Emperor, AIR 1930 Lah 171 (Tek Chand and Fforde JJ.).
150. *Supra* n. 142.
151. Mt. Bhukin *v.* Emperor, AIR 1948 Nag 344 (Hemeon and Sen JJ.).
152. *In re* Kuruba Chinna Hanumakka, AIR 1943 Mad 396 (King and Kuppuswami Ayyar JJ.).
153. Minai *v.* Emperor, AIR 1938 Nag 318 (Grille and Digby JJ.).
154. *Supra* n. 151.
155. *Supra* n. 152.

realise what she was giving him since she had a motive—another man—to commit the crime.[155]

Where there were women-accused, the oft-iterated defence of grave and sudden provocation advanced in crimes of violence has had to give way to a defence of ignorance of consequences, and motives of reviving deteriorating relationships in the home.

XIV

Nestling in the creases of the cases, we find courts acknowledging the provocation of sustained abuse. In the variations on 'slow burn', anger and hurt at the betrayal by the wife/mother in her role as such wife/mother has given a reasonableness to the provocation leading to the crime.

The 21 year old was "admittedly" a woman of evil reputation unanimously denounced in common talk of the village as being "a very bad character." There was no doubt that she "was a woman who was leading an immoral life while living in the house of her husband."[156]

One day, as her husband left home for work, he asked her "not to be very often absent from home." "In reply she abused (him) who, according to the rough ways of the people of his class, gave her a shoe-beating accompanied with abuses." When she abused him further, the "exasperated" husband picked up a stick which "unfortunately happened to be lying handy, (and) gave her a couple of blows one of which proved fatal."[157]

"(I)n judging the conduct of the accused," the court said. "One must not confine himself to the actual moment when the blow . . . was struck. . . . We must take into account the previous conduct of the woman. Her evil ways were the common scandal of the village and must have been known to the husband, causing him extreme mental agony, shame and humiliation. . . . It must have undoubtedly irritated and

156. *Supra* n. 153.

157. Jan Muhammad *v.* Emperor, AIR 1929 Lah 861 (Broadway and Agha Haidar JJ.).

annoyed him to a degree when in answer to his veiled remonstrance and injunction to her to mend her ways, the woman started abusing him. Like the last straw which breaks the camel's back, we may take it that a point was reached when the unfortunate husband lost all self-control . . . "[158]

In a lucid description of slow burn, the court said ". . the whole affair should be looked at as one prolonged agony on the part of the husband which must have been preying upon his mind and led to the assault upon the woman, resulting in her death."[159]

Considering too that that it was "extremely unlikely that the husband would have gone beyond the stage of shoe-beating" if the stick had not been lying there, the conviction was altered to the lesser charge of culpable homicide, and the sentence reduced from transportation for life to 10 years' RI.[160]

There is the "extremely sad" case of the 30 year old soldier of "unblemished character" that the court narrates for its readership.[161] There was nothing to indicate that he was "a man of a violent or vindictive character." Yet, when once they went to the Jhelum to have a bath, he confessed, "he first immersed (his wife) in the water and then pushed her to a spot where the water was beyond her height." Thereafter, he lodged a complaint against another for enticing his wife away—a futile attempt to conceal the truth.

The Magistrate, when recording his confession, "went out of his way to suggest to the accused that if he had killed a faithless wife after all he had not done anything very heinous and should save his own life."

His confession "was a voluntary statement . . . (and) contained the whole history of the unhappy married life of the accused and how he tried hard to reform his erring wife without any Success." And from the confession, the court found that the "woman apart from being an unfaithful wife, was also a thief. She took away the ornaments and clothes

158. *Ibid.*
159. *Ibid.*
160. *Ibid.*
161. *Ibid.*

which had been entrusted to her by her husband to her lover." Then, he 'confessed', "when she was living with (him), she abstracted a sum of Rs. 20 from a box with the intention of leaving him and joining her lover in her native village."[162]

In this manner did the husband accused of murdering his wife "confess" to the unchastity and thievery of his wife, in mitigation of his crime.

He was convicted not for the offence of murder, but of attempted murder. Forgiving of the wronged husband who had killed his wife, the court said, "Having regard to the protracted sufferings of the accused through the obstinacy, viciousness and flagrant immorality of the deceased", the sentence was reduced from 7 years' imprisonment to 3 years.[163]

"This is a tragic case," said the court when a lad of 19 murdered his mother.

The boy's father had died about 15 years before the incident. His mother had since lived in concubinage with one KP. The boy "confessed" that his mother had settled all her property on KP, that he had been asking her for a long time for his share and his brother's share and also asking her to arrange for his marriage. "He complained that far from agreeing she would not even cook for him. . . . When she refused to cook for him that morning," it was said, "he stabbed her in front of his house."[164]

Recommending treatment in a Borstal institution in preference to a long-term of imprisonment, the court held, "There has been no sudden provocation in the present case but long and sustained provocation which resulted in a complete breakdown of control."[165]

It seems probable that the court was seeking mitigating circumstances to deal with what it perceived to be "this very

---

162. *Supra* n. 148.
163. *Ibid.*
164. *Ibid.*
165. *In re* Periyaswami Asari, AIR 1949 Mad 223 (Govindarajachari and Mack JJ.).

difficult case of criminal psychology." Yet, there is the court's statement that "(t)he appellant has been the victim of an abnormal and unnatural environment bereft of maternal affection . . ."[166] which both implies slow burn and the reasonable expectation of a woman, the absence of which may justify condoning violence to her person.

XV

The sati of Sampati Kuer when she was 20, had been married for 10-12 years during which time she had continued in her father's house, and went to her husband's only to nurse him when he fell ill till he died, happened in 1927. It appears the marriage was never consummated. She was a "pious, gentle Hindu girl of high caste." She was pardanashin . . . "she had no father"; "she had no sufficient male protection—only a weak-minded superstitious boy brother."[167]

The story as recorded finds the police using persuasion and threats to prevent the sati. The overpowering of the police by the family of the dead one, Sampati's brother and the"fanatical mob" was followed by the young widow seating herself on the pyre. A conjurer's trick was employed to set her on fire. "At the torture of the flames the poor creature leapt from the tire and rushed into the river.. . . Some police put out in a boat and tried to rescue her. They were threatened...; she was told to drown herself."[168]

However, the police did manage to get her ashore. For two days and two nights she lay there in agony before she died. The doctor and the police, trying to relieve her agony, were driven away. For, when she lay under the tree, there began that "which was the first fruits for which the Pandes had been waiting, a stream of coins to flow which they greedily picked up."

The relation of the event points to murder all the way, but it was unlawful assembly and abetment to suicide which

166. *Ibid.*
167. *Ibid.*
168. Emperor *v.* Vidyasagar Pande, AIR 1928 Pat 497 (Courtney Terrell CJ and Adami J.).

were the charges. And punishment was prescribed accordingly.

In a passage in conclusion, the court said, "This is our judgment firstly that such evildoers may be punished; secondly, that an innocent girl may be avenged so far as we can avenge her; and, thirdly, in order that those who will not learn by reason may be taught by fear." And continued: "I do not pretend to know if there be any survival after this life is finished, but if so and if god be just and merciful in the sense that we very imperfectly understand justice and mercy, then such of these men as survive their earthy punishment may well go on humble pilgrimage to Sampati's shrine and with ashes on their heads cast themselves down and invoke her gentle spirit to intercede with the almighty to save their guilty souls from everlasting damnation."[169]

* * *

So ends a saga in sati that started in marriage.

XVI

We leave the wife behind and enter the grey area of prostitution in law which has occasionally emerged to be argued in the courtroom.

A keen tussle to establish the validity, or otherwise, of the adoption of a daughter by a dancing woman of the prostitute class is reported. When the Penal Code made buying and selling of a minor for purposes of prostitution a crime, some argued, it controlled private law, and adoption of a daughter by a dancing woman would be invalid. A judge would however say that adoption in Hindu law was "allowed partly for continuing the family and partly for securing a person competent according to thc custom of the caste to perform the funeral obsequies of the adoptive parents and to take their property." Adoption in the case of dancing girls should not therefore be "confounded with prostitution which is neither its essential condition nor necessary

---

169. *Ibid.*

consequence, but an incident due to social influences."[170] "The policy of the Penal Code," he said, "...is not to obliterate altogether the line of distinction between the province of ethics and that of law, but to protect the chastity of minors and to assure them the freedom of choosing married life when they attain their age, whether they are the natural or adopted daughters of dancing women, and to leave otherwise the incidents of their legal status as daughters untouched, whether the parties concerned are dancing women or ordinary Hindus."[171]

This statement of the special status of prostitute woman apparently had a reiterative resonance, for, again : "as a matter of private law it must be taken, the class of dancing women being recognised by the Hindu law as a separate class having a legal status, the usage of that class, in the absence of positive legislation to the contrary, regulates rights of status and inheritance, adoption and survivorship."[172]

Where it was found, as fact, that the adoption was with the "intention of prostituting the adopted daughter even while she was a minor", particularly after the Penal Code was brought into effect in 1861, the adoption would not be valid.[173]

All these discussions and decisions were in the Madras High Court. The Bombay High Court's view was that adoption of a daughter by a dancing woman of the prostitute class was invariably to promote prostitution, and so opposed to public policy.[174]

In the case which ranged over these decisions it was held that the presumption that the adoption would be for the purposes of prostitution was "rebuttable." As there was evidence "that it is customary among dancing women of

---

170. *Ibid.*

171. Muttusami Ayyar, J. in Venku *v.* Mahalinga (1886) 11 Mad 393 quoted in Duggirala Veeranna *v.* Duggirala Sarasiragnam, AIR 1936 Mad 639 (King and Menon JJ.).

172. *Ibid.*

173. Muttusami Ayyar and Parker JJ. in Muttukannu *v.* Paramaswami (1889) 12 Mad 214 quoted in Duggirala *supra* n. 171.

174. Duggirala *supra* n. 171.

Mandapata village to which the parties belong, to adopt girls for the purpose of giving them in marriage to others", the adoption was recognised was valid.[175]

A study in contrasting concerns and presumptions is witnessed where a husband demands restitution of conjugal rights, and his 'wife' denies there was any legal marriage between them. She alleges that "she was brought by her father to the plaintiffs house (when she was about 16) after the death of her grandmother and made to live there by her father and was subjected to various kinds of torture and ill-treatment by the plaintiff and her father", and that she was "ultimately compelled to lead a life of prostitution."[176]

A motor driver gave evidence before the court that he had visited her on three occasions. The court said, simply, "I do not believe the evidence of this witness." When another witness, a plumber, said that he had seen her being compelled by the plaintiff to lead an immoral life, and that she was always subjected to ill-treatment and assault, the court again merely said, "I also disbelieve the evidence of this witness." She said she had asked a neighbour—with whom she later moved in—to report to the police and that he had said it was not his business to do so. But the court said that, all available evidence suggested that "if" her story was true, "she had ample opportunity of complaining about the conduct of her father and the plaintiff and could have easily obtained protection and could have left the plaintiff'. The "story" of the woman, the court said, was "so highly improbable that no court should attach any weight to it."[177]

Why this disbelief?

"I can hardly conceive that a father would degrade his only child at the age of 13 or 14 by taking her to the house

175. Mathura Naiken *v.* Esu Naicken (1879)4 Bom 545; Hira Naikin v Radha Naikin (1913) 37 Bom 116 and Girimallappa Channappa Samsagar *v.* Kenchava San Yellappa Hosmani 1921 Bom 270 (Macleod CJ and Fawcett J.) referred to in Duggirala *supra* n. 171.

176. *Ibid.*

177. Gokuldas Waghaji *v.* Lutchmi, AIR 1937 Rangoon 308 (Sen J.).

of a Gujarati for the purpose of living on the earnings of her prostitution."[178]

Perhaps this presumption dominated the decision.

The part prejudice plays engaged the court's attention when PD appealed against her conviction and sentence under Section 8 of the Calcutta Suppression of Immoral Traffic Act 1923. PD was Lakshi's mother. Lakshi was 13. An anonymous letter set in train an investigation and prosecution, charging PD with having brought her daughter to Calcutta from Rangoon to carry on the business of a prostitute. PD protested that her daughter was a musical artiste of some repute. There was evidence of her engagements which led the High Court to say that it was "tolerably clear and indeed beyond doubt that this girl Lakshi was a skilled and attractive performer as a singer and dancer who had already made good in her profession." But the Chief Presidency Magistrate, convicting PD had said: "But the fact remains that hers is a dual calling. It is perfectly obvious that her profession as a cinema actress does not militate or clash with her other less reputable calling." And, again: "Another circumstance worth noting is that the girl is not a cinema actress but only a singer and dancer who performs in cinema theatres. It is well known that singing and dancing constitute the advertisement side of prostitution."[179]

The High Court explained the prejudice : "It may be that actresses and actors in this country are still regarded as persons who are not respectable just as in England in the middle ages they were deemed to be rogues and vagabonds." And added, "but it does seem to me even so that it is carrying the matter a little too far to suggest that the carrying on of a profession of a singer or dancer by a woman does necessarily and of course connote the business of prostitution." The mother was then given the benefit of doubt, and acquitted.[180]

---

178. *Ibid.*
179. *Ibid.*
180. Parbati Dasi *v.* Emperor, AIR 1934 Cal 198 (Costello and M.C. Ghose JJ.). For an instance of the presumed sexual licence of a cinema actress, see *supra* JJ. 14.

When prostitute women were sent into virtual exile by municipal bye-laws, they didn't take it lying down. We witness the rare sight of women accessing courts to assert their rights of residence. Sometimes it was when a bye-law specified the area within which prostitute women were permitted to reside—they were otherwise exiled. They then argued that this area was "a busy market area not far from the centre of a large city, an area which may be suitable for a few wealthy members of the profession, but difficult of access to numbers of unfortunate prostitutes who are for this reason practically prohibited from residing in the municipality. And the court held that, under the law, there was power in the Municipal Board of Agra "to make a bye-law prohibiting prostitutes from residing in specific areas or area, but not (to) make a bye-law prohibiting them from residing in the whole of the municipal area with the exception of a certain specified part."[181]

Then, another judge in another case disagreed with this interpretation, and sent it up for consideration by two judges. Now these two judges disagreed with the earlier decision.[182] Their view was that, since the municipal limits were determined, and the exceptions to the rule that public prostitutes could not reside or ply their trade were specified, the law—which required that the area from where they were to be excluded be specified—stood satisfied.[183]

It was in another aspect that the bye-law incurred judicial displeasure. The bye-law excluded prostitute : women who already owned houses in the prohibited area; it was only future acquisitions of property which were targeted. It was this "invidious distinction" which met with the court's stern disapproval, and caused it to strike down the bye-law.[184] It is in another similar situation that the court's central concern becomes clear: The Municipal Board, the court suggested,

181. *Ibid.*

182. Mt. Muhammadi *v.* Emperor, AIR 1932 All 110 (Kendall J.).

183. Mt. Naziran *v.* Emperor, AIR 1932 All 537 (Sulaiman and Young JJ.).

184. *Ibid.*

"would be well-advised to re-draft this bye-law so as to make it of general application."[185]

Even if it is to recommend that all prostitute women be sent into exile, we do here hear the language of equality being used- a reasonably rare occurrence, certainly where women are concerned.

"All the world over," a court said elsewhere,[186] "some women take to the life of a prostitute either from choice or by force of circumstances." "Public prostitute," as the court defined her, "is a woman who usually and generally offers her person to sexual intercourse for hire and who openly advertises and acknowledges her occupation by word of mouth, deportment or conduct." And it is a "great deal of moral degradation alone (which) will attract the application of a drastic law which involves the consequence of a woman being compelled to leave her house in which she might have invested her fortune or might have other associations." Recognising citizenship in the woman, the court remarked : "The Municipality is entitled to make bye-laws with a view to preserve order and decency; but the bye-laws must be strictly construed where they trench upon the rights of a citizen." Reading her rights so, the court held that the Municipal Board could not treat the girl as a public prostitute "simply because she belonged to the caste of prostitutes or that her mother and mother's sisters were public prostitutes."[187] This, despite an inevitability expressed in its comment: "In view of her antecedents and environments, it may not be difficult to make a forecast of the plaintiffs (who was a singing girl) future life."[188]

The "unfortunate woman",[189] as we see, was not a passive entity in the judicial process. It was not paternal protection, or admonition, that reached the woman in prostitution, though there were manifestations of disbelief

185. *Ibid.*

186. Mt. Chanchal *v.* Emperor, AIR 1932 All 70 (Sulaiman J.).

187. Municipal Committee, Etah *v.* Mr. Asghari Jan, AIR 1932 All 264 (Sen and Niamatullah JJ.).

188. *Ibid.*

189. *Ibid.*

about the role men played in inducting the women into prostitution, and keeping them there. She may not find herself silenced into a passivity which is the consistent condition of the wife. There is, instead, a certain agency recognised in her interaction with law and with the state. Perhaps their other-than-ordinariness when the court referred to "dancing women or ordinary Hindus",[190] and their identity as a "separate class having a legal status"[191] gave them a position denied to the wife in the arena of law.

XVII

The incremental construction of the Reasonable Woman and the Reasonable Man is done. It is only left now to draw out a description of the Reasonable Woman and the Reasonable Man.

The Reasonable Woman is a wife.

She becomes one with the family of her husband.

She is sexually available to her husband.

She doesn't expect to be treated as a wife; only to be maintained. She is entitled to shelter and safety, though she is not entitled to stay in her matrimonial home.

She has no marital honour, so she cannot encash her honour as her husband can.

She does not put obstacles in the path of her husband marrying another wife.

She goes to another man only when her husband does not support her. And she cannot reasonably claim to be maintained by two men.

She is chaste and keeps unsullied the bed of her lord, even when he deserts her.

She may, in the occasional case, have a share in her husband's salary, but she cannot use it to maintain her mother.

She belongs to a generally her father or her husband.

190. As the prostitute woman is euphemistically termed in *supra* n. 146 at p. 20.

191. *Supra* n. 171.

She is married young.

She does not exercise choice.

She has no politics.

She is incapable of being a legal guardian.

She does not have children; she bears her husband children.

Her worth is reckoned on the capitalised value of her usefulness to the man.

She does as her husband would have her do. She does not roam about, but stays at home, cooks and takes care of the children.

She does not complain of rape.

She is incapable of being dishonoured, especially if she is of a low caste and the assault is by a high caste man.

She does not answer back. She does not retort even if she is incorrectly and publicly accused of carrying on a relationship outside her marriage.

She is not a cinema actress, or a singer, or a dancer: she is a dependent.

An actress, not being a Reasonable Woman, has no right to reticence in being medically examined to demonstrate her virginity.

The Prostitute Woman is not a Reasonable Woman, and is not to be judged as a Reasonable Woman would.

* * *

A pause at marriage before we launch into a discovery of the Reasonable Man: Marriage is a necessity. The state is vitally interested in keeping a marriage going. It is only rare and exceptional cases which may convince the court to accept the inevitability of divorce. In any event, divorce is not a legal necessity.

* * *

The Reasonable Man gets married and gets a dowry for it.

May be he marries again.

He chastises his wife in moderation, perhaps with small beatings. But he doesn't cut his wife's nose.

He may murder his wife if he catches her in adultery, but he is not to murder for one who is not his wife, such as his mistress, concubine or one to whom he is engaged.

A Reasonable Man confesses to his wife's infidelity, thievery and adultery.

He has control over his wife, and his daughter.

He knows that he becomes a procurer if he encourages his daughter to return home from ill-treatment and suffering with a promise to find her another husband.

He demands damages from the adulterer when his wife is in an adulterous relationship, and asserts his power of legal possession. But he does not make profit out of his wife's dishonour.

He is entitled to custody of his wife, even if she has not yet reached puberty. If he can't have her in his possession, he has her sent away from her mother into an institution.

He does not steal another man's wife; he respects another's property; even if he doesn't treat his own property well.

Prolonged agony may cause him to kill.

* * *

Reasonable Expectations span the distance between the Reasonable Man and the Reasonable Woman.

3

Human Rights Lawyering: A Feminist Perspective

Nandita Haksar

I

I am a product of both the feminist and the human rights movements that emerged in our country in the post-emergency period. These coincided with the international upsurge in democratic consciousness beginning in the 1960s with the civil rights movement in the USA, the students' movement in Europe, and the rise of the ecological and feminist consciousness in the 1970s. It was a time when questions were raised about the meaning and significance of all aspects of our lives.

I joined law after we realized the need for feminist lawyers because of our frustration in trying to make other lawyers understand the need to translate our politics into legal action. However, after the initial years I was a full-time human rights lawyer. Thus, I was lucky to be a part of the rich debates in both these movements but often found that the discussions in each took place in ignorance of the discussions in the other movement.

I do not think I will be able to capture the excitement of those heady days when we spent hours discussing each word and trying to redefine the meaning and content of concepts from the point of view of our politics. These debates were invariably and unashamedly linked to questions of ethics and morality. And that is what gave the movements their depth and their reach. Here I will deal with some specific questions that arose in the course of the two movements which touch the problems of international human rights standard setting.

I do not think that these debates can be understood unless we remember the context and the background of the debates. And then we can appreciate the real problems involved in evolving a jurisprudence which is relevant to our people's rights.

II

In a way it all started in 1979 with the Supreme Court judgment in the Mathura rape case. The judgment would perhaps have gone unnoticed if it had not been for four law teachers who lodged their strong protest against the judgment by writing an Open Letter to the Chief Justice of India. These four teachers were: Upendra Baxi, Raghunath Kelkar and Lotika Sarkar of the Delhi University and Vasudha Dhagamwar of Poona. The letter dated September 16, 1979,[1] criticised the judgment of Justices Jaswant Singh, *Kailasam and Koshal in Tukaram* v. *State of Maharashtra*,[2] which reversed the High Court verdict holding two police constables guilty of raping a 14-year old tribal girl in the police station.

The letter quotes the judgment on the facts:[3]

Immediately thereafter Ganpat . . . took Mathura . . . into latrine situated at the rear of the main building, loosened her underwear, lit a torch and stared at her private parts. He then dragged her to a chhapri. . . . In the chhapri he felled her to the ground and raped her in spite of her protests and

1. Reproduced in (1979) 4 SCC (Jour) 17.
2. (1979) 2SCC 143.
3. *Supra* n. 1 at p. 17.

stiff resistance on her part. He departed after satisfying his lust and then Tukaram . . . who was seated in the cot nearby, came to the place where Mathura . . . was and fondled her private parts. He also wanted to rape her but was unable to do so for the reason that in a highly intoxicated condition.

The main focus of the Open Letter is the interpretation of "consent in the law of rape." The Supreme Court held that Mathura had submitted to the rape. Therefore, the policemen were not found guilty of rape. The letter pointed out that "Consent involves submission; but the converse is not necessarily true. Nor is absence of resistance necessarily indicative of consent . . . From the facts of the case, all that is established is submission, and not consent. Could not their Lordships have extended their analysis of 'consent' in a manner truly protective of the dignity and right of Mathura? One suspects that the court gathered an impression from Mathura's liaison with her lover that she was a person of easy virtue. Is the taboo against pre-marital sex so slag as to provide a licence to Indian police to rape young girls? Or to make them submit to their desires in police stations?"[4]

The Open Letter said the judgment was in sharp contrast to the judgment of the court a year ago in which Justice Krishna Iyer condemned the practice of calling a woman to the police station as a gross violation of Section 160(1) of the Criminal Procedure Code, 1973. But in that case the woman was Nandini Satpathy, Chief Minister of Orissa. The law teachers ask 'The court, under your leadership, has taken great strides for civil liberties in cases involving affluent urban women (e.g. Mrs. Maneka Gandhi and Mrs. Nandini Satpathy). Must illiterate, labouring, politically mute Mathuras of India be continually condemned to their pre-constitutional Indian fate?"[5]

The Open Letter asked that the matter be re-heard by a Full Bench as they had done earlier in cases relating to the right to property, because this case had raised important issues relating to "human rights of women under the law and the Constitution."

---

4. *Id*. at p. 20.
5. *Id*. at p. 21.

Women's organizations demanded a review and the court said they had no *locus standi* (legal standing) to represent Mathura. We were outraged. In fact our predominant feeling was that we were asking for justice for ourselves, not for an unknown girl in a village in Maharashtra. I do not think that it was a coincidence that the issue of *locus standi* should have first come up with the women's groups who so intensely identified with the victim. As feminist lawyers we would refuse to take a case on behalf of a man against a woman. We were told we were violating our professional ethics. We were told under the Bar Council of India Rules we could not refuse to accept any brief. This refusal undermines the basic principle of rule of law and civil liberties ethics, i.e., that everyone is presumed to be innocent till proved by a fair trial to be guilty. As one barrister writes "if the advocate is unwilling to act for the alleged rapist, why is he willing to act for the alleged drug-dealer, or by-batterer, or drunken driver? Once the principle of acting for all those in court is sacrificed, there is no logical stopping place other than a subjective test of representing only those the advocate does not find too reprehensible in the light of the charge which they face and upon the strength of which it is the task of the court to adjudicate."[6]

The Rule presumes that the courts and the law are equally capable of giving justice to the accused rapist and to the victim. But this is exactly the presumption that the feminists challenged. They said the courts and the law were heavily weighted against the raped victim, especially if she was poor.

However, the problem remains and there is a conflict between human rights ethics and feminist ethics. This came out sharply several times when several senior advocates who were Presidents of civil liberties groups took up cases on behalf of the accused rapist; in at least two cases the accused was a policeman.

6. David Pannick, Advocates, Oxford University Press, Oxford, 1992, pp. 144-45.

While as a human rights lawyer I have taken up cases on behalf of people with whom I have serious political differences but the case involved some problem of violation of human rights, I would not take up a case to defend a rapist or a person accused of being one. But then one friend, and an activist, asked, "If I was accused of rape by the state in a false case would you not take up my case?"

Well, this friend was arrested outside the Supreme Court on the charge of being a Naxalite. And the other side lawyer did go around saying that he was a rapist. Some lawyers even made insinuations that I had special interest in doing his case. After all why was I so agitated and involved? I told this to the Judge in the open court and at least that time the other side lawyer withdrew from the case out of embarrassment. Such was the moral strength of our movement in those days.

As a feminist and as a human rights lawyer I take up cases in which I am intensely involved. In the beginning I was told in a variety of ways by a variety of colleagues that this was "unprofessional" behaviour. We must not get too involved. My answer to most is that they are intensely involved in making money while my priority was the emotional satisfaction of extending solidarity to the accused. When lawyers do legal aid or *pro bono* cases they provide an important service, but it is essentially an act of charity. A human rights lawyer's involvement is an act of solidarity and the political difference between charity and solidarity is vast.

While the issue of representation is still open, the issue of *locus standi* was resolved in 1982 when the Supreme Court gave a detailed judgment recognizing the right of concerned citizens and of NGOs to represent the oppressed or exploited people in public interest cases. However, the small victory won has once again been circumscribed.

III

The debate on reforms of the law of rape involved many issues. One of the demands made by many women's groups was the demand for an in-camera trial. The women had good reason to make this demand because the experience of the rape victim in an open court was invariably one of humiliation. She was made to relive her trauma bit by bit under humiliating cross-examination as a court full of men enjoyed the spectacle. It was this experience that forced some of the women's groups to demand that rape trials be held in-camera and that the rape victim's name not be published or broadcast by the media to save her from further stigma.

These two demands undermined both the basic principle of a fair trial, that it be held in open court and the right to freedom of expression and speech. There was great controversy and heated debate over these issues both among women's organizations and within those sections involved in the law reform process. The government asked the Law Commission to look into these demands.

The Law Commission in its 84th Report, submitted in 1980, went into various questions relating to "Rape and its Allied Offences Some Questions of Substantive Law and Procedure." The Commission weighed the pros and cons of the demand for an in-camera trial in the light of the fact that an open court is an essential ingredient for a fair trial. The report quotes from a pamphlet brought out by the National Council for Civil Liberties in the UK[7] that the law should recognize the fact that there is still a stigma attached to rape from which the victims may suffer for years afterwards.

However, the Law Commission goes on to state that "we would wish to extend this view to include the stigma that may attach itself to the accused for years afterwards even following an acquittal. In this context it should be remembered that the making of an allegation of rape against any man imposes upon him an equally unpleasant, humiliating and embarrassing experience . . . ."[8] and so he is entitled to the same protection as the alleged victim.

And so the recommendation for in-camera trial was not for the protection of the woman but the man. Section 327 of

7. On the Rape Controversy, National Council for Civil Liberties, 1975.
8. 84th Report of the Law Commission, On Rape and Allied Offences, Controller of Publications, New Delhi, 1980, p. 29 (emphasis supplied).

the Code of Criminal Procedure, 1973 stipulates that the trial should be in an open court where the general public should have access to it. The section was amended in 1983 to provide for in-camera trial in the case of rape and further it was stated that where any proceedings are held in-camera "it shall not be lawful for any person to print or publish any matter in relation to any such proceedings, except with the previous permission of the court."[9]

While many women's organizations welcomed this recommendation, the feminists were not comfortable with the idea of censorship. They conceded that "(t)he question of rape and publicity, however, is complex and needs to be discussed in some detail. It is true that much of the sensational reporting such cases receive tends to glamorise the rapist and romanticise the victim, perpetuating the cult of rape." However, after weighing the various arguments the women's organizations who had gathered together for the national conference in Bombay in 1981 passed the following resolution against in-camera trials:

> We feel this is a direct attack on the ability women's organizations have to organize on the issue of violence against women. The danger extends further, because, on the pretext of protecting women, the Bill is in fact a blatant attempt to impose press censorship, which assumes significance in the context of increasing atrocities and repression of people's movements. We therefore resolve we will defy this provision of the Bill if it is passed by Parliament, as women, we will support each other's defiance, specially by unitedly protecting our alternative media.

The government drafted the Criminal Law (Amendment) Bill, 1980 on the basis of the Law Commission's recommendations and the Bill was referred to a Joint Committee of Parliament. Many members expressed their disagreement with the proposal for the banning of any

9. *Ibid.*

disclosure of the victim's identity. However, in 1983 it became an offence to disclose the identity of the victim in a rape trial under Section 228-A of the Indian Penal Code, 1860.

Just after these amendments to the rape law which included other questions which also have a bearing on civil liberties, such as the reversal of burden of proof and definition of a category of rape as custodial rape, there as a heightened awareness among feminists to take greater care about articulation of demands in case our arguments are used by the state to curb civil liberties. In the process we soon discovered that we would have to evolve a new jurisprudence.

IV

In December 1983, a magazine called India 2000 carried an article by Salman Khurshid (then an advocate practising in the Supreme Court, later a Minister) criticising the reforms in the rape law. He called the Open Letter "preposterous" and stated that the letter had sparked off "an extremely distasteful public agitation." He made a series of defamatory statements about Mathura calling her "a somewhat precocious and certainly sexually forward girl" and the facts of the case as being "fishy."

Salman Khurshid failed to quote even one paragraph from the Open Letter. He did not point out that the Supreme Court judgment did not have a single word condemning the use of a police station as a theatre of rape or submission to sexual intercourse. Apart from the objections we had to the contents of the article we had as much objection to the illustrations that went with it and to the cover photo. The question before us was that while we wanted to support the magazine and the individual writer's right to freedom of speech and expression, we wanted some sanctions against them for biased and anti-women writing and the accompanying photos and illustrations.

The only law in India under which we could have taken the editor and the writer to the courts was the law against obscenity. Obscenity is an criminal offence under

Sections 292 and 293 of the Indian Penal Code. [The Indecent Representation of Women (Prohibition) Act, 1986 came three years later]. Feminists involved in the media did not want to use the obscenity law since they felt it was the law under which great works of literature such as novels by D.H. Lawrence and stories of Sadat Hasan Manto had been banned.

Besides, the right to freedom of speech and expression has been so long denied to women that it is the dearest right for a woman who wants to break the barriers of silence imposed on her by the family, society and the outside world. The first thing we all learnt in the women's movement was to speak out. We learnt that it was not wrong to vent our feelings and that suffering humiliation in silence is not dignified.

In fact our smallest acts of rebelling against society's mores and customs, like wearing a dress or jeans was termed as indecent and obscene. Women were denied knowledge of their own bodies since all talk of sex was deemed to be indecent and depiction of explicit sex was obscene. This was not true for India only, but also for the so-called advanced West. For instance, a woman's magazine Spare Rib was banned in Ireland because it showed women how to examine their breasts.

After considerable debate we decided to file a case against India 2000 and Salman Khurshid in the Press Council of India for a violation of professional ethics. We said that the illustrations were pornographic. We made a sharp distinction with the law of obscenity which was "aimed at suppressing explicit description or discussion of sex except for religious or scientific purposes. The underlying assumption is that sex depraves and corrupts people unless it is confined to the legitimate areas of laboratory or hospital. that is, there is something pathological about sex."[10]

On the other hand, we said:

10. Letter by Nandita Haksar, Prabha Krishnan, Sujata Madhok and Nina Kapoor, India 2000, January 1, 1985.

> Pornography in its essence is the celebration of indignity and degradation of women. For pornography projects women in a violent and depraved way and endorses their subjugated status in a patriarchal world.

The petition went on to say that the ubiquitous marketing of pornographic images engenders in all women a sense of defeat and powerlessness and in all men a sense of exultant power. To fight such forces as these, to seek to create a world where such images will cease to titillate and sell is not to interfere with anyone's freedom, but to ensure justice for that powerless section which holds up half the Indian sky.

The Press Council heard our arguments but refused to make any distinction between obscenity and pornography. It is ironic (or perhaps not so) that India's Porno King, Harbhajan Singh, the publisher of India's pornographic magazines Hotwave and Confidential Adviser, was a member of the Press Council when it heard the case. The editor, however, agreed to publish our rejoinder which was carried in its January issue.

Western feminists have also been battling with the problem of balancing their support for the right to freedom of speech and expression with their demand for state regulation (which could include banning magazines, etc.). They have argued that censorship of sexually explicit material appeared to be 'dependent on a kind of prudishness or moralism. The conflict was thus between freedom of speech on the one hand and attempts to prevent offensiveness to the community on the other.[11] For instance, the demands made by the BJP women's groups for banning the beauty contest on the ground that Indian women should not wear swimsuits since it was against Indian culture.

However, the regulation of pornography is demanded not on the basis of offensiveness but in terms of gender-

---

11. Cass R. Sunstein, "Pornography, Sex Discrimination and Free Speech", in Larry Gostin (ed.), Civil Liberties in conflict, Routledge, London and New York, 1988.

related harms. Feminists argue that pornography is a reflection of, and a perpetuator of, inequality on the basis of gender, inequality that is manifested in discrimination of various sorts and in sexual violence. According to the feminists pornography both sexualizes violence and defines women as sexually subordinate to men. In fact, pornographic materials feature rape, explicitly or implicitly, as a fundamental theme.

The Preliminary Report of the UN Special Rapporteur on Violence Against Women made these observations on the effects of pornography:

Pornography is perhaps the extreme manifestation of media violence against women. Although this question involves important issues concerning the right to freedom of expression, the portrayal of violence against women in pornographic literature and film, where women are shown bound, battered, tortured, humiliated and degraded, is a major problem for those confronting violence against women in their societies.

Pornography is both a symptom and a cause of violence against women.

Pornography in itself violates female dignity but, in addition, it often promotes attitudes and practices which result in violence being directed against women.

While a majority of people in the civil liberties movement would concede that pornography is a kind of discrimination against women, many have not supported the demand for government regulation on the ground that the argument could extend to covering many books and films which are also responsible for negative portrayals of other communities.

One writer argues that there "is actually nothing which ought to distinguish pornography itself from other constitutionally protected speech. Although Dos Kapital is indeed different in form from a centerfold in Hustler magazine, rational discourse should not be treated as a matter of law superior to even the rawest of emotional appeals."[12]

---

12. Barry Lynn, 'Pornography and Free Speech: The Civil Rights Approach", in Larry Gostin *supra* n. 11 at p. 173.

This argument is not as frivolous as it seems at first reading. Around the time the article was written, the United States government was trying to deport feminist author Margaret Randall for the political content of her publications, using the McCarran Walter Act which allowed the deportation of non-citizens "for any number of ill-defined ideological crimes."

Margaret Randall was at that time (around 1986) a fifty-two-year old mother of four children and internationally, acclaimed author of more than 40 books, prescribed by many courses in women's studies and Latin American Studies.[13]

The problem with all such discussions is that they do not see the liberal model of human rights as problematic. The basis of human rights model is the right to equality to all, or the equal protection to everyone under the law. Thus under this model the feminist, pornographer and the Nazi are equally protected but not anyone called a communist—as we see in Margaret Randall's case. The latter does not get protection because he or she challenges the basis of liberal ideology.

Parallel to the debates on the freedom of speech and expression with regard to pornography has been the debate within the civil liberties groups on the right of freedom of speech and expression for racists and fascists. In the infamous Skokie case the American Civil Liberties Union did defend the right of a Nazi to freedom of speech. Writing on this decision, an ACLU member said:

> At the core of genuine feelings of rage and despair inspired by the Nazi demonstration at Skokie (a Jewish inhabited area) was a wish that the Nazis would disappear, that the kind of evil they exemplify would cease to exist. Most of us share that hope but preventing Nazis from speaking will not exorcise them. They will continue to speak racial hatred wherever they are. Is it not better to expose this venom and to

---

13. David Cole, "What's a Metaphor?: The Deportation of a Poet", 1(1) The Yale Journal of Law and Liberation, 1989, p. 5.

> respond to it, rather than drive it underground to fester? The best defence against hateful speech is counter-speech upholding democratic values which appeals to the good sense and decency of the people.[14]

The debate in India has not been very sharp and even democratic sections very easily support the banning of books and even parties. Often this demand for a ban is a substitute for the other, harder, option of building a movement for an alternative vision. The women's movement has too often stopped short by articulating demands only in terms of changes in the law. In contrast was the vision of the early socialist feminists in India. For instance, on the issue of rape, even before the Open Letter a fact-finding group of feminists had gone to investigate an incidence of mass rape in the Santhal Parganas. They discovered that rape was being used in the rural areas by the police "as a weapon of class domination."

In a paper entitled "Rape as a form of state reprisal in peasant movements", two of the feminists presented their findings to the National Conference of Women held in Bombay in 1980. They said that rape is "not just another atrocity to be condemned, but an act of political violence."

They went on to explain that:

> The general pattern of peasant struggle and its repression in the Santhal Parganas is a familiar one; Santhals attempt to reclaim their land by forcibly harvesting it; the mahajans, its illegal landlords, call in the CRP (Central Reserve Police); the CRP and the mahajans follow the Santhals into their villages and embark on a grand voyage of plunder, arson, and rape (the men have either run away or are rounded up and arrested-warrants are no where to be seen). This pattern is one we have seen all over rural India— sometimes even in the working class areas such as

---

14. Norman Dorsen, "Is There a Right To Stop Offensive Speech? The Case of the Nazis at Skokie", in *supra* n. 11 at p. 133.

> Bailadilla (M.P.). What singles out the Santhal areas is that in an immediate sense it is Inc women who bear the brunt of the repression, that this fact has not been recognized by the parties who work in the area, and no programme of defensive resistance is as yet being constructed though such incidents have been everyday ones since 1978 which is when the movement for forcible harvesting got under-way.[15]

In sharp contrast to this perspective in which the vision of the socialist feminists was to link the women's issues to other struggles is the individual case based approach that has emerged as reflected in the report of the National Meeting of Women's Organizations "Against Rape" in April 1990. The overwhelming concern here is with working out legal definitions of rape and description of individual cases. Although the report states that the "attempt was always to keep the issue of rape in its political and economic ramifications, at centre-stage", it miserably failed to do so.

The Report states that the media is important in "rendering men more accountable by putting the rapist in the limelight" but it could also sensationalise rape. There is no mention of pornographic materials. By the end of the last decade the pornography industry generated an estimated seven billion dollars a year with pornographic films outnumbering others by three to one.

V

Without a sharp political understanding of issues, we can easily fall in the trap of the American Civil Liberties Union's stand of defending pornography on the ground of freedom of speech. In an attack on ACLU, two feminists responsible for drafting anti-pornography legislation in the USA said:

---

15. Radha Kumar and Shoba Sadagopan, "Rape as a form of State reprisal in peasant movements", presented at National Conference of Women at Bombay in 1980.

> "The ACLU's stated commitment is to protect the Bill of Rights ...not pornography as such, though it's hard to tell sometimes. Without a commitment to real equality of the same magnitude as its commitment to those first ten amendments, the ACLU defends power, not rights. No matter how notorious the exploitation, as for instance in child pornography, the ACLU ends up substantially defending those who exploit the powerless. The ACLU demands a literal reading of those first ten amendments, especially the First Amendment, especially its speech provision. This is an exceptionally conservative position both philosophically and politically and it has a conservative political outcome: it keeps already established patterns of inequality intact. . . .

The ACLU refuses to accept responsibility for the fact that in the Unit States speech has to be paid for in money. The ACLU defends the power of corporations who own and control the means of speech against the aspirations of dissidents who have been excluded from the circle of protected speech by sex or race.[16]

The liberal human rights model is based on primacy of individual civil liberties over all rights. And the Indian feminists have often fallen into the trap of accepting this model and articulating their demands in terms of individual civil rights for women. Thus often women's rights have seemed to be in contradiction with the rights of minorities. The question is whether women's rights are necessarily in conflict with the rights of minority Communities?

I shall give one illustration of how this emphasis on individual liberty has created a false dichotomy between

---

16. Andrea Dworkin, Pornography and Civil Rights, Organising Against Pornography, A Resource Centre for Education and Action, Minneapolis, Minnesota, 1988; Catherine Mackinnon, Pornography and Civil Rights: A New Day For Women's Equality, Organising Against Pornography, A Resource Centre For Education and Action, Minneapolis, Minnesota, 1988.

women's rights versus tribal peoples' rights. Liberal feminists have been attacking customary laws among the tribal peoples in the North East on the ground that it is patriarchal. It does not treat men and women equally. They by implication look upon the customary law as "traditional" and compare it to legislation. At a purely superficial level this stand is absolutely correct from the tribal women's point of view. And it is also true that some of the tribal women facing anti-women customs which deprive them of their basic rights have also joined in the demand that the customary law must go.

Thus we see that the same women's groups (including some feminists) are asking for a uniform civil code in the North East even though they have stopped demanding this for the rest of India ever since the slogan was taken over by the Hindu communal forces. They now see that their dream of a uniform civil code can be imposed on the peoples of the North East in the name of upholding women's rights.

Within this perspective the only way a woman's organization can intervene is by supporting the demand for the codification of tribal laws, and for the anti-women customs to be declared violative of Article 14. And that is precisely what some of the women's groups have been advocating. All this seems logical and consistent with the slogan that women's rights are human rights.

But international human rights law also recognizes the rights of indigenous people to their way of life and in case of the Nagas this is protected by Article 371A of the Indian Constitution. The Article protects Naga social and religious practices and their customary law and procedure. In addition just a few years ago the world celebrated the Year of the Indigenous People. How do we see this contradiction?

The Vienna Declaration on Human Rights of 1995 has a special section on indigenous peoples' rights. Article 31 states that the World Conference on Human Rights urges States to ensure the full and free participation of indigenous people in all aspects of society, in particular in matters of concern to them. And the customary law would certainly fall in that category.

Thus some activists are inclined to give primacy to the rights of the community and the rights of indigenous people over the rights of the individual tribal woman. This approach comes easily to those sections within the Third World who have in the process of attacking the primacy of individual rights within liberal theory gone on to give primacy to socio-economic rights. This stand has the effect of sacrificing vital civil and political rights and even justifying their violation in the name of some "larger" principle, which may be community, nation or State.

VI

Can we think of a third model of human rights? A model which gives equal importance to individual and collective rights? I think we can. But it requires that we build a jurisprudence which would question the premises upon which the present human rights and some kinds of feminist jurisprudence are based. We have to create new human rights.

But the contemporary Indian feminists have not (with a few exceptions) really produced a critique of the law without which it is not possible to evolve a new jurisprudence. In fact they seem to have accepted a premise of the liberal theory that rule of law can guarantee human rights and, by extension, women's rights. In a draft on law reforms some feminists state that "the law has to provide more rights and equality than the society itself . . . the law also has to be forward-looking and progressive."

The human rights movement in India has through its work over more than Iwo decades shown how oppressive the state is. Through its continuous fact-finding efforts it has built up a systematic critique of the Indian State which leaves no room for doubt that the law is primarily an instrument for conservation and perpetuation of the present social, economic and political inequality and injustice. Human rights literature all over the world bears testimony to the fact that the law in a liberal state is not at all a neutral and objective arbitrator of rights. In fact, in the guise of protecting rights the law protects power.

Legal ethics which are supposed to uphold the dignity of the profession are also meant in fact to mystify the real role of the law and the lawyer in maintaining *status quo*. The law is anti-poor, anti-women and casteist. It is not only a question of wrongful implementation but the inherent intent of the statute.

If we understand this we see that the existence of an alternative legal system assumes a very important role in showing us that there are other ways for dispute settlement than the so-called modern legal system. It is in this context that the fight of indigenous peoples all over the world, including in India against the imposition of the alien legal system on them assumes a Special political significance.

In fact what is derogatively or rather patronisingly called tribal Customary law is in fact tribal jurisprudence. I do not mean to either mystify this system or romanticise it but having studied some aspects of it, I can say that tribal jurisprudence has evolved ways and means of preserving the ecological balance and preventing ecological degradation by evo lag Complex sets of practices which form a part of their jurisprudence.

Central to their jurisprudence is the concept of collective rights to natural resources and the concept of common property. It also balances the rights of the individual with that of the community in ways that caste-based communities do not. For the purpose of this article I need not go into the details of the law except to say that tribal societies are based on common property and collective rights. If these are eroded the whole society would be destroyed.

The Indian State knows this very well. And that is why it has encouraged the slogan for the codification of the tribal laws. They say that in order to implement them they need to be written down. However, the problem is not only of writing them down but of codification. Once any customary law is codified it will get fossilised and die a natural death because it will not be able to evolve. By defining tribal customary laws as "traditional" the state makes out that its relevance is historical, and it takes away the right of the tribal people to evolve their customs in accordance with the times.

In fact, tribal laws have been evolving over the times. In Mizoram, Nagaland and in Meghalaya (I do not know of the other States) I know of many instances when the customary law has been used to solve complex issues, including interventions in student movements or inter-village disputes. It is also true that there are powerful vested interests within their societies who do not want custom to change or misinterpret it in order to serve their narrow personal interests. For instance, the Chief Minister of Nagaland who said that reservation for women would be against the traditional society.

Women in the North East could in fact fight for the right to evolve their own customs in consonance with the times. The student movement and the civil rights movements would support their efforts to a large extent. But this would mean reading and understanding their own society with a new perspective. It is a far more difficult task than filing a petition under Article 14 or getting the support of women who have no stakes in the future of tribal societies.

This path would not lead to a confrontation between women's rights and rights of indigenous peoples as much as the second approach. Unfortunately women from the middle classes, whether in tribal society or non-tribal, have used the women's movement for either solving their individual problems without any commitment to a larger movement or to get into the same patriarchal structures which are the cause of oppression.

Many of us have seen that the language of the feminist movement has changed from human rights to expediency. Just as upper caste and upper class women began using the movement to get the right to participate in the very system they had said was exploitative and oppressive, tribal elite women are using the movement to get rights to become a part of their own system which they say is patriarchal.

We have already seen how the demand for a uniform civil code has been usurped by the Hindu communal forces. For the women involved in the national movement it was a demand linked to secular, modern and rational politics of nation-building. The insensitivity of the feminists to minority rights and feelings of Muslims was an important reason for the success of the Bhartiya Janata Party in communalising our demand. Some feminists have been equally insensitive to the problems of tribal peoples in the North East and their patronising attitude can be used by the state to justify the breaking up of the North East societies by imposing an alien legal system based on individual liberty and private property.

Such disintegration of those societies is taking place for many other reasons but the women's movement can be a powerful legitimiser. The government wants to liberate the land from the peoples' control for developmental projects which will lead to further landlessness and impoverishment of the people.

Some years back a similar controversy came up in the context of land rights of Ho women in the heartland of Jharkhand. A fact-finding team had gone to inquire into a police firing and reports of police atrocities in Singhbhum district of Bihar. The committee was sponsored by the All India People's Union for Civil Liberties and Manushi, a women's magazine. The team included Madhu Kishwar of Manushi and in the course of the fact-finding she found that Ho women suffered greatly because of the denial of land rights to them. She decided to challenge this discrimination against women under the Chotanagpur Tenancy Act, 1876. The petition challenged the provision as a violation of Articles 14 and 15 of the Constitution read with Article 46 of the Directive Principles of State Policy.

The petition prayed that in order that these fundamental rights become meaningful in the lives of Ho women it would be necessary that the provisions of the Succession Act, 1925 apply to the Ho people. At a superficial level there is nothing objectionable about the contention that Ho women should not be denied the benefit of the equality clause in the Constitution and be given the right to inherit property. The petition is based on the classical human rights arguments.

When I say classical human rights I mean the first generation rights which include the right to be treated equally under the law, that the law apply equally to all citizens and that any discrimination must be based on valid classification. Let us examine each of these rights in the context of the petition filed by Madhu Kishwar.

The Constitution and international human rights law also recognize the right of tribal peoples to be given special protection. Thus, there are different sets of laws which apply to tribal peoples and to non-tribal peoples. And Section 76 which Madhu Kishwar seeks to have deleted is the section which constitutes the major part of the CNT's concern with and defence of the Adivasi land system. Without this section the Act becomes merely an assurance of rent free holding of those few remaining sections of land registered as bhumihari and khuntkatti.

"The remainder of the Act, which forms its major portion, consists in a defence of non-Adivasi rights in land, e.g. the rights of superior landlords. Thus the role of the Act in defending the tribes becomes subverted, its power to defend tribal tenancy becomes destroyed, when Section 76 is deleted."[17]

The Adivasi land system is based on a communal land system in which no one has absolute rights to land, in a system of common property the people have mainly a right to use the land rather than private property rights of absolute ownership. This is true for a majority of the land systems in the North East. If the Indian Succession Act was introduced it would mean the government and other vested interests would use it to break common property into private property, since the Succession Act, 1925 does not recognize common property or use rights.

Then we come to the question of the discrimination between men and women. There is no question that it exists within Ho and other tribal societies. However, the position of women within tribal societies is far better than the position of women in caste society. There is equal availability of divorce to both men and women, there is a right to remarry, absence of religious taboos concerning menstruation and absence of physical seclusion. The sense of human dignity and self-respect is the basis of tribal societies.

---

17. Hazel Lutz, Questions Relating to the Movement to Grant Tribal Women Equal Rights in Land (Unpublished). Also see Madhu Kishwar *v.* State of Bihar (1992)1 SCC 102.

By inviting the Supreme Court's intervention into the affairs of the Ho community and asking the Supreme Court judges to evaluate their society is in many ways similar to what happened in *Shah Bano's case,*[18] when the judges were invited to interpret the Holy Koran.

The destruction of tribal societies means the destruction of ways of life, philosophies and traditions which are a rich source of cultures which teach values based on co-operation, rationality and consensus, in contrast to the capitalist values of competition, elections and conflict. When I say this it does not mean that I am advocating the "preservation" of these societies in museums. Nor do I think that we can revive the past. What I am saying is that there are alternatives to filing writ petitions on grounds of violation of human rights or fundamental rights; there are other ways of dealing with the problem of inequality between men and women in tribal societies.

VII

What are these ways? First of all there is a need to build a movement based on tribal socio-cultural traditions. It is not possible to discuss these political strategies within this space. But an alternative to a movement cannot be a petition. I strongly feel we should resort to the law only when the movement is strong enough to carry the law reform forward. In almost all such cases a legal battle should only supplement the political battle outside the courts. If the legal battle is allowed to take precedence over the political one the law is easily used by the state to subvert the political battle's objectives.

Having said this I feel that we do need to build a movement for creating a new jurisprudence which draws on the human rights law and certain feminist legal critiques. But both human rights jurisprudence and liberal and radical feminism place a great deal of stress on individual rights and

---

18. Mohd. Ahmad Khan *v.* Shah Bano Begum (1985) 2 SCC 556:1985 SCC(Cri) 245.

the primacy of individual liberty over all other kinds of human rights. Already Western feminists have found the limitation of this approach. For instance, Carol Smart writes that while the language of rights was important in challenging the conservative order in the past for women and other oppressed sections she feels that "the rhetoric of rights has become exhausted, and may even be detrimental. This is especially the case where women are demanding rights which are not intended (in an abstract sense) to create equal rights with men, but where the demand is for a 'special' right (e.g. women's right to choose) for which there has been no masculine equivalent."[19]

I would add that the rhetoric of rights is also not useful wherever we need greater state protection and regulation. In such situations human rights arguments can be and have been used to deny women's rights. An extreme case is of the United States government's refusal to ratify the Convention on the Elimination of Discrimination Against Women on the ground that it invites greater state regulation in "private" areas which is against their Constitution.

The conflict between individual rights and collective rights is inherent in human rights law. And this conflict is specially relevant to the women's movement and also to the other movements concerned with equality of races and rights of the other oppressed groups. It is also important for those engaged in a struggle for workers and peasants rights. In fact, trade unions have forced the international human rights law to recognize the right to collective bargaining. It is a recognition of a modern community right and not a traditional one. Article 29 of the International Bill of Human Rights also recognises that "(e)veryone has duties to the community in which alone the free and full development of his personality is possible."

In this effort to construct a new jurisprudence we can draw upon the human rights tradition, the feminist critiques of law and on tribal jurisprudence. But we cannot hope to

19. Carol Smart, Feminism and the Power of Law, Routledge, London, 1989, p. 139.

begin this task without a political understanding of our society and economy and without a vision of a future society. If our vision is limited, so will be our legal strategies. It is not an easy task. But then nothing worth doing is or has been easy. There lies the challenge.

4

Feminism in Indian Legal Education

ARCHANA PARASHAR

INTRODUCTION

I like to think of myself as a feminist and since I am employed as a legal. Academic my professional persona is that of a legal feminist. I feel strongly about the place of feminism in the education system and feel fortunate that I have the opportunity to contribute some ideas. However, my ideas and opinions as well as the ability to formulate and articulate them are largely a result of my coming in contact with some exceptional feminist teachers during my education.

The path of my professional development was moulded by my exposure to feminist ideas and I often marvel at the coincidence that I met with such good feminist teachers. It is this good fortune which makes me determined to argue for a legal education that does not depend upon simply meeting up with the right teachers. The argument of this essay is that legal feminism should form an integral part of legal education and not be treated as an idiosyncrasy or a luxury provided to some but not a law students. I wish to argue that feminist theory is relevant for understanding all legal theory and to do that adequately it is crucial to reconceptualise legal education. One of the fundamental tasks is to give a central place to the significance of gender (and all other differences) as an analytical concept in legal analyses. My conception of legal education is that, as other education, it is empowering and that this power should be used to strive for a just society. Specifically, I wish to address the increasing disillusionment of some Indian feminists with law and argue that it is premature to give up an engagement with law in the struggle to end oppression of women and the aspiration for social justice.

The essay is divided into four broad parts. In the first. section 1 will discuss the context of the debate about the relevance of engaging with the legal system as a feminist goal. In the second part I will examine the contemporary critiques of law and assess the distinctiveness, if any, of legal feminist critique. The third section will examine the structure of legal education. In the final section I will explore the rationales for changing the content and method of legal education. I will also develop a tentative proposal for a foundation course on legal theory.

LAW REFORM AS A FEMINIST GOAL

The context of this essay is the increasing disenchantment with law reform by feminists in India and in the first world countries. The bases of both these views are however, very different and have serious consequences for legal feminism in India. The Indian feminist movement from the very beginning targeted law reform as the strategy for changing the conditions for women. The disenchantment with law reform of some Indian feminists arises partly due to the practical problems they face: despite many law reforms in the last few decades women continue to be severely oppressed in India. This has prompted some feminists to change the focus of feminist activity from law reform to seeking empowerment of women in more immediate ways, i.e. employment opportunities, education, health and access to medical services, etc. While this change in priorities is understandable I argue that it is happening without much serious attention to the theoretical and normative significance of the role of law in maintaining 5 or alleviating the oppression of Indian women specifically.[1] I believe that this is where the role of appropriate legal education becomes most obvious. Legal academics have to engage in these analyses in order to address the criticisms of feminists but more importantly legal feminists have to better equip the coming generation of lawyers—law students, practitioners, judges, policy-makers, researchers and academics—to explore the role of law in maintaining oppressive *status quo* or in achieving social justice for all sections of society. This task of Indian legal feminists is made difficult by a narrow conception of legal education.

It is further complicated by the trend in first world feminisms to de-emphasize law reform as a solution to the oppression of women. The legal status of women in first world countries in conjunction with the improvements in their economic and social conditions allows first world feminists the luxury to disregard law reforms since they no longer yield sufficient returns.[2] But the same is not true for most women in third world countries and they cannot afford to forego the changes even at the very modest level of incremental legal rights. But women and particularly feminist legal writers are confronted with contemporary western feminist analyses that portray engagement with law reform as naive at best. Therefore, I wish to address my argument to all legal feminists and emphasise that feminists in the first world countries equally bear the responsibility to develop truly inclusive legal analyses. It may be asked at this point why should developments in first world feminisms be of any significance to a discussion on Indian legal education. My answer is that it is undeniable that what happens in Indian universities is inextricably linked to theoretical trends in the first world universities. You can call it anything-continuing imperialism of thought, post-colonial condition or

1. See for example, Nivedita Menon, "Rights, Law and Feminist Politics: Rethinking Our Practice", in Swapna Mukhopadhyay (ed.). In the Name of Justice, Manohar, New Delhi, 1998, pp. 15-41.
2. For a good discussion of the reasons why all feminists must involve themselves with issues not directly relevant to them see Linda Alcoff, "The Problem of Speaking for Others", 20 Cultural Critique, 1991, p. 5.

globalisation—but the fact remains that the so-called third world thought is influenced and shaped in relation to European and North American theoretical developments. The problem, however, is that trends in European and North American thought are culture and context specific. Whether the theoretical claims are universalistic, or more recently Post Modernist efforts at non-universalism, they are not simply extendable to third world societies. Yet the scholars in these societies are expected to 'work' with such developments. This is well illustrated by the example of legal feminist theory: the first world legal feminists simply do not concern themselves with the problems faced by third world women. There is some feminist literature by third world women situated in first world countries or by post-colonial writers in first world countries but invariably they write about the experiences of being an expatriate or migrant.[3] However, the feminists in third world countries do not have the option to ignore the developments in first world feminist theory.

The situation is further complicated by the conventions of judging arguments as scholarly only when they conform to the rules of academic writing and of course these rules are a codification of the membership of the powerful and prestigious centres of knowledge.[4] While those working in west countries can safely ignore. The writings and concerns of third world academics the same option if exercised by third world writers makes their work less meritorious and only

3. For example, Gayatri Spivak, In Other Worlds: Essays in Cultural Politics, Methuen, NY, 1987: The Post-Colonial Critic, Routledge, London, 1990: Outside in the Teaching Machine, Routledge, NY, 1993, Chandra Talpade Mohanty, "Under Western Eyes: Feminist Scholarship and Colonial Discourses", 30 Feminist Review, 1988, p. 61; see also Mohanty, Third World Women and Time Politics of Feminism, Indiana University Press, Bloomington, 1991.

4. For a similar but not exactly the same example see the debate between minority scholars and the establishment scholars in American legal writing, Alex Johnson Jr., "The New Voice of Color", 100 Yale Law Journal, 1991, p. 2007. This article gives an overview of the debate generated by Randall L. Kennedy, "Racial Critiques of Legal Academia", 102 Harvard Law Review, 1989, p. 1745: see also "Colloquy", 103 Harvard Law Review, 1990, p. 1844.

because the issues identified by them are not important for the dominant discourses including first world feminisms.

When first world feminist theory argues that reliance on law reform is insufficiently theorized, that it is a mistaken focus, or that true understanding of women's oppression lies outside of law, it places every third world feminist in a double bind: she is confronted with arguments not applicable to her context yet she has no option to ignore them. It is true that first world feminism is not a unified theory and among western feminists there is a robust debate going on about essentialism in feminism. The existence of this debate shows a concern with accommodation of differences. But my concern is that these issues are mainly raised by African-American feminists and are specific to their context.[5] The post-structuralist feminist theorists have sought to accept the challenge of making feminism genuinely pluralistic but these analyses have their own set of problems, i.e. their high level of abstraction, the disjuncture between radical discourse and political action.[6] Moreover, I argue that they are as ethnocentric as any other theory. For all their efforts at eschewing universalistic claims of meta theory the post-modern theorists' rite as if their ideas are simply extendible to everyone and everywhere.

A debilitating but continuing aspect of colonization (which is now given the more palatable title of globalisation) most thinkers in third world countries have to deal with western ideas and institutions. Whether the ideas are about capitalism, democracy, rights discourse, feminism or legal systems. all of them are western in origin.[7] Thus even though Indian legal feminists are free to develop their own analyses

5. See for example, Angela Harris, Race and Essentialism in Feminist Legal Theory", 42, Stanford Law Review, 1990, p. 581; Patricia Williams: 'Alchemical Notes: Reconstructing Ideals from Reconstructed Rights', 22 Harvard Civil Rights and Civil Liberties Law Review, 1987, p. 401.
6. See for a comprehensive discussion Ben Agger, Gender, Culture and Power Toward a Feminist Post-modern Critical Theory, Praeger, London, 1993.
7. Philip Altbach, The Dilemma of Change in Indian Higher Education,

they have to constantly engage with the ideas of western legal scholars, feminists or otherwise and position themselves in relation to these ideas. The transfer of institutions is a complex and ongoing project that does not come to an end with the formal end of colonial rule.[8] The former colonized polities have very little, if any, option to abandon the institutions introduced by former colonizers. The point is not whether such turning back of the clock is desirable or undesirable but the more limited assertion that it is impossible. However, it remains the exclusive burden of the third world thinkers to keep in touch with the developments in mainly European and American thought while the first world writers go on as if third world societies did not exist and certainly did not matter for the purposes of their theories.[9] There is a loose parallel between the predicament of third world feminists *vis-a-vis* first world feminisms and the relation between western feminist thought and mainstream theories. Feminism has to keep positioning itself against the developments in mainstream ideas and even now it is common to characterize feminist theory as special interest theory rather than acknowledging it as a critique of the foundations of the mainstream theoretical project.[10]

---

in Suma Chitnis and Philip G. Altbach (eds.), Higher Education Reform in India: Experience and Perspectives, Sage, New Delhi, 1993, p. 1 at p. 28.

8. This issue is not studied so much; see William B. Hamilton (ed.), The Transfer of Institutions, Duke University Press and Cambridge University Press, London, 1964.

9. See for example 'Archana Parashar, Reconceptualisation of Civil Society, Third World and Ethic Women', in Margaret Thornton (ed.), Public and Private: Feminist Legal Debates, Oxford University Press, Melbourne, 1995, pp. 221-42. I was once again struck by this feeling when reading Ulrich Beck, Risk Society: Towards a Modernity, Sage, London, 1992.

10. The issue has most recently surfaced in the rise of post-modern genre of writing and feminists efforts to theories in similar ways. The inter-relation between the developments in mainstream and feminist theory is variously described, i.e., that post-modernist developments are external to feminism or that they are mutually supportive where feminisms have appropriated and developed the

Ideally I would like to see the conventions of theory building modified to be genuinely inclusive and all feminists to take responsibility for all women but in the meanwhile the predicament of Indian feminists need not be completely paralyzing. They can and ought to synthesise their experiences and knowledge with the ideas present in western feminist thought and thus create genuine third world feminist theory. And it is by reference to these ideas that Indian feminists should decide whether law reform can be abandoned even as a strategic move. To do otherwise would amount to acting without sufficient understanding of the situation, either because there are no appropriate third world feminist analyses available, or by applying western theories which do not have any relevance for the Indian situation. Therefore, in the following section I argue that Indian legal academics ought to develop feminist analyses of law specific to India and other third world countries. This project can be best carried out as a reconceptualisation of legal education in India. But before developing this argument I believe a clear understanding of the claims of distinctiveness of feminist legal theory is a prerequisite.

FEMINIST LEGAL THEORY

Feminist legal theory is a development similar to that of feminist analyses in various other disciplines. Feminisms have challenged the basic social structures and the hierarchies they legitimize. The feminist writers have chronicled the pervasiveness of the hierarchy of gender, initially by showing how various disciplines had left out women from their descriptions and analyses and more radically to point out the flaws in the fundamental assumptions in the methods and theories of various disciplines.[11]

---

post-structuralist and, post-modernist ideas. In either case it is important to point out the links between feminist and non-feminist strands of contemporary social, political and cultural theory. M. Barret and A. Phillips, Desumbilizing Theory: Contemporary Feminist Debates, Polity Press, Oxford, 1992.

11. Examples of such challenges can be taken from every discipline. For a representative work see Sue Rosenberg Zalk and Janice Gordon-

The link between feminist movement and the law goes back at least to the early suffragette demands that disparities between the formal rights of men and women should be eradicated.[12] The initial focus of feminist writings on the law was to identify how legal rules either stopped short of treating men and women as equals or when formal equality was granted how such rules were manipulated to prevent women from exercising their rights. Very soon it became obvious that mere formal right to equality did not result in actual equality between women and men and what was needed was a reconceptualization of the categories of analysis.

The more recent analyses of law by feminists have thus focused attention on the institution of law. Rather than examining specific laws these analysts examine the nature of the legal system and argue that law is one among many institutions of a hierarchical society. It is anything but an autonomous system and is implicated in maintaining patriarchal relations. The distinctiveness of such feminist legal analyses lies in that they use gender as the explanatory concept to expose the bias of the so-called neutral norms.[13] Feminist analyses thus challenge the universality of concepts used in legal theory and have moved beyond the simplistic demand that the equal protection of law be extended to women as well.

The distinctive achievement of feminist critique is that it has exposed the function of public/private distinction in legal theory.[14] It is commonplace in Liberal legal theory to use the public/private division to justify restricting the reach of

---

Kelter (eds.), Revolutions in Knowledge, Feminism in Social Sciences, Westview Press, Boulder, 1992; Sandra Harding, Whose Science? Whose Knowledge?: Thinking From Women's Lives, Open University Press, Buckingham, 1991.

12. See for example, Mary Wollstonecraft, 'Vindication of the Rights of Women', excerpted in J. Cooper and S. Cooper (eds.), The Roots of American Feminist Thought, Allyn and Bacon Inc., 1973, pp. 15-50.

13. For an introductory overview see Frances Olsen (ed.), Feminist Legal Theory, Vols. I & II, Dartmouth, Aldershot, 1995.

14. Margaret Thornton (ed.), Public and Private: Feminist Legal Debates, Oxford University Press, Melbourne, 1995.

law to the public sphere only. The idea of freedom as a consequence is conceptualized as freedom from governmental control. Feminist authors have shown that this notion of freedom only holds true for men and not for most women.[15] The origins of analytical distinctions between the personal, political and economic spheres may be explainable as useful for abstract analyses but the consequences of relying on such concepts to produce analyses are very different for men and women.[16] Thus an argument is made for the need for gender specificity of analytical concepts.

The implications of the demand for gender specificity in legal theory are: firstly, that interconnection of public and private spheres indicate the pervasiveness of women's oppression in all spheres of life because masculinity is privileged at the expense of femininity and the role of law in maintaining such a division is not benign; secondly, trial rather than accepting the traditional domain of jurisprudence to be just philosophy of law and treating law as an autonomous, neutral and universal institution it would be much more realistic to examine the connections between law. economy and society. The specific contribution of feminism is that it has demonstrated that interdisciplinary study of law can still remain biased. Traditional Marxist analysis moves away from the autonomy claims of the law and demonstrates the link between a specific kind of economy and a particular type of law. Parallel to this the Weberian sociological analysis explains the rise of modern law as a specific kind of rationality.[17] In neither case is there any mention of gender differences. Therefore, feminists have argued that it is essential to incorporate gender as an important aspect of law to build appropriate legal theory. I wish to emphasize that feminists claim that gender is a relevant explanatory concept for any theory.

---

15. Carole Pateman, Sexual Contract, Polity Press, Oxford, 1988.
16. Linda Nicholson, Gender and History: The Limits of Social Theory in the Age of Family, Columbia University Press, Columbia, 1986.
17. Max Rheinstein (ed.), Max Weber on Law in Economy and Society, Harvard University Press, Cambridge, Mass, 1954.

If the neutrality claim of the law is flawed and feminists argue that gender is not only a matter of difference but of hierarchy[18] the next question is whether a truly neutral perspective is possible. Feminists have argued that 'perspective scholarship' is inevitable.[19] This is a much wider claim as it points out not only bias against women but the inevitability of all knowledge being informed by some perspective. This development has also been described as the post-modern turn in feminist theory.[20] A major implication of this development for legal feminism is whether inevitability of bias or perspective leads to relativism, that is gender issues are no more relevant than any other difference like race, age, class *et al.*[21] This issue is of central significance for my argument because if feminist ideas should inform legal education should not all differences be considered relevant? My answer is yes, but without ignoring gender specificity. That is, gender should be conceptualized as not only constructed by one's sex but a complex interplay of factors which go into constituting notions of masculinity and femininity.[22] But there is scope for also acknowledging the hierarchy of gender and avoid falling into the trap of formal equality, that is, since both genders are constructs both are to be treated on par. Otherwise it would amount to legal theory being gender neutral once again, only in a new garb.

In my view the whole purpose of post-structural feminist analysis is to examine how privilege is created and

---

18. Catherine Mackinnon, Toward a Feminist Theory of the State, Harvard University Press, Cambridge, Mass, 1989.
19. Martha Fineman, "Feminist Theory in Law: The Difference it Makes", 2 Colombian Journal of Law, 1992, p. 1 at p. 10; Kimberlie Williams Crenshaw, "Foreword: Toward A Race-Conscious Pedagogy in Legal Education", 11 National Black Law Journal, 1989, p. 1; Nicola Lacey, "Feminist Legal Theory Beyond Neutrality", 48 Current Legal Problems, 1995, p. 1.
20. Linda Nicholson (ed.), Feminism/Post-Modernism, Routledge, New York, 1990.
21. See Linda Nicholson, Social Post-Modernism: Beyond Identity Politics, Cambridge University Press, Cambridge, 1995.
22. Sandra Lee Bartky, Feminism and Foucault, Northeastern University Press, Boston, 1988.

exercised and if the ultimate aim is to dismantle privilege[23] feminist theory does not have to claim the primacy of gender oppression, but neither does it have to ignore the hierarchies maintained through complex interactions of notions of superiority on the basis of race, class, gender et al. There is ample scope for post-strucfural feminists to avoid relativism and work for creating a genuinely plural theory. Nor is there any reason to hierarchise differences[24] and feminisms ought to be understood as concerned with non-oppression of not only women but of everyone.[25] It is this understanding of the significance of feminist analyses that I wish to use to argue for reconceptualizing legal education. But before that in the following section I will discuss the assumptions on which much of contemporary legal education is structured.

LEGAL EDUCATION

In this section I will discuss two interrelated issues: whether the content and methodology of legal education is dependent upon the ideas about the nature of law, i.e. is it an autonomous system or one amongst many institutions of society: and whether professional *versus* academic aims of legal education are necessarily divergent.

Legal education in India and in much of the industrialised world is premised upon the idea that law is an autonomous institution. The study of this autonomous institution is best carried out in an autonomous discipline. Thus law students need only concern themselves with : study of law as if it did not have any connection with other institutions and disciplines. In Indian law schools (as in overwhelming number of western countries' law schools) the

---

23. Henry A. Giroux, "Post-Colonial Ruptures and Democratic Possibilities: Multiculturalism as Anti-Racist Pedagogy", 21 Cultural Critique, 1992, p. 5.
24. This point is made with eloquence by Arthur Brittan and Mary Maynard, Sexism, Racism, and Oppression, Basil Blackwell, London, 1984.
25. Deborah Rhode, "Missing Questions: Feminist Perspectives on Legal Education", 45 Stanford Law Review, 1993, p. 1547.

connection between law and society is ignored and at the most jurisprudence or the philosophy of law is the only theoretical knowledge necessary for lawyers-defining what is valid legal knowledge at the very start.[26] The idea that legal knowledge is specialised knowledge best acquired by studying the doctrine of law is the foundation of much modern legal education but it has a very long history.

In the common law countries legal education bears strong resemblance to its pattern in the United Kingdom. Initially, in Britain, legal training was only professional training available to apprentices in the Inns of Courts.[27] For a long time it has been a contentious issue whether legal education has a place in the academy or the university system. At the base of this contention lies the conception of law as a profession or an academic discipline. The origin of this question may be traced to the differences between common law and civil law countries' conception of law and legal education. Civil law countries followed the traditions of Roman law and organised the study of law in the universities. On the other hand, Britain and thereafter all common law countries denied the influence of Roman law and attributed special characteristics to common law. The custodians of this special knowledge were the practitioners therefore, there was no point in studying law at universities.[28]

---

26. See for discussion of the issue whether jurisprudence is the only theory necessary for legai education, N. MacCormick, "The Democratic Intellect and the Law", 5 Legal Studies, 1985, p. 172; Alan Hunt, "The Role and Place of Theory in Legal Education: Reflections on Foundationalism", 9 Legal Studies, 1989, p. 146; William Twinning, Law in Context: Enlarging A Discipline, Clarendon Press, Oxford, 1997, at p. 113 argues that there is a distinction between legal philosophy and legal theory as the latter is much broader but nevertheless a legitimate enterprise.

27. Philip Anstie Smith, A History of Education Far The English Bar, with Suggestions as to Subjects and Methods of Study, Butterworths, London, 1860, p. 1; William Twinning, *supra* n. 26, at p. 7 cites The Robbins Report on Higher Education (Cmnd 2154: 1963) which does not mention law, and The Report of the Heyworth Committee on Social Studies (Report Cmnd 2660: 1965) notes that the study of law has been mainly concerned with training barristers and solicitors.

28. See for a discussion of some of these issues Patrick Kavanagh,

Robert Gordon[29] discusses the rise of the idea in the United States that law is a technical science and the study of law is independent of all other social actions and norms. Thus the classical positivist model describes law as a science without any political, social or moral content.

In contemporary times legal education is part of the university system in all countries in Europe and North America but the tension now is manifested in disagreements about the content of legal education. Clive Walker says that in England the demands of legal professional bodies shape legal curricula.[30] He also observes that a sharp divide persists between the liberal/contextual and vocational/technical approaches to legal studies.[31] In Australia the divisions between these perspectives are discussed in the Pearce report.[32] In India the Indian Bar Council is primarily responsible for defining the shape of legal curricula.[33]

"Legal Education and The Foundationalisation of the University", 5 Australian Journal of Law and Society, 1988-89, p. 11.

29. Robert W. Gordon, "The Case for (And Against) Harvard", 93 Michigan Law Review, 1995, p. 1231 at 1245.

30. The same is true for Australian legal education. Recently the Priestly requirements of eleven core courses have been adopted by all Law Schools. See L.J. Priestly (Chair of the Consultative Committee of State and Territorial Law Admitting Authorities), Uniform Admission Requirements: Discussion and Recommendations, 1992.

31. Clive Walker, "Legal Education in England and Wales", 72 Oregon Law Review, 1993, p. 943 at p. 944 and 950. See also, Cyril Glasser, "Radicals and Refugees: The Foundations of the Modern Law Review and English Legal Scholarship", 50 Modern Law Review, 1987, p. 688; David Barnhizer, "Freedom To Do What? Institutional Neutrality, Academic Freedom and Academic Responsibility", 38 Journal of Legal Education, 1988, p. 346 esp at p. 353.

32. Tertiary Education Commission, Report of the Committee to Review Australian Law Schools: A Discipline Assessment, 1987, Australian Government Public Service. See also the special issue on Legal Education of 5 Australian Journal of Law and Society, 1988-89.

33. Amrik Singh, "Coordinating Agencies in Higher Education", in Suma Chitnis and Philip G. Altbach (eds.), *supra* n. 7 at p. 207. See for a discussion of the constraints under which legal scholarship is produced in India, Rajeev Dhavan, "Means, Motives and Opportunities Reflecting on Legal Research in India", 50 Modern Law Review, 1987, p. 725.

In my opinion the two issues, of the nature and content of legal education are linked and must be discussed together. In the USA the predominant model of legal education is one involving the study of judgments or cases.[34] This is called the case method and is followed in India as well, in particular by the Law Faculty of Delhi University. With very few exceptions the content of legal education is primarily court judgments, and a study of these judgments allows a student to acquire knowledge of common law doctrine, precedents and statutes.

The case method focuses attention on the appellate court judgments which the students may or may not study in the Socratic style. Nankivell[35] says that Australian law schools have adopted the case method without accepting the Socratic model of teaching. He argues that case method shifts the focus of study from secondary materials like treatises to primary materials—the court judgments. But the Socratic method requires a further shift—from exposition by the teachers to directive questioning so that students themselves arrive at formulations of legal principles. He says this is not possible when teachers simply give lectures.

Much of the recent debate in legal scholarship is concerned with the accuracy of the claims of legal theory about the rule of law and the principled nature of law. In their own ways legal realists,[36] critical legal scholars[37] and law

---

34. Robert B. Stevens, Law School: Legal Education in America from the 1850s to the 1980s, University of North Carolina Press, Chapel Hill, 1983.
35. Ross Nankivell, "Legal Education in Australia", 72 Oregon Law Review, 1993, p. 983, at p. 991; Michael Chesterman and D. Wiesbrot, "Legal Scholarship in Australia", 50 Modern Law Review, 1987, p. 709.
36. Laura Kalman, Legal Realism at Yale, 1927-60, University of North Carolina Press, Chapel Hill, 1986.
37. Duncan Kennedy, "Legal Education and The Reproduction of Hierarchy: A Polemic Against the System", in D. Kairys (ed.), The Politics of Law, Pantheon Books, New York, p. 40; cf Catherine Hantzis, "Kingsfield and Kennedy: Reappraising The Male Models of Law School Teaching", 38 Journal of Legal Education, 1988, p. 155: "Symposium on Critique of Critical Legal Studies by Minority Community Scholars", 22 Harvard Critical Race and Critical Legal Theory Law Review, 1987, pp. 294-447.

and society critics[38] challenge or deconstruct the claims about the details of legal doctrine. I wish to argue that legal education must broaden its scope of inquiry beyond the details of doctrine. The role of law in contemporary societies can only be understood if law is acknowledged to be an institution interdependent with all the other institutions of society. A fundamental requirement for such a reconceptualization of legal education is that study of law be made genuinely interdisciplinary.

There are already well established traditions of studying sociology of law, history of law, law and economics, law and anthropology *et al.* All these perspectives have an important role in explaining the nature of law but all of them are discipline specific. For example. the issues discussed by a sociologist of law are different from those chosen by an economist studying law. But for a legal scholar it cannot be enough to examine one aspect of law and not another. Richards argues that in asking for interdisciplinarity it is not suggested either that law schools should develop 'Law and . . .'[39] approaches or that law should be studied in other departments. Instead the law's 'deepest interpretive study must be in the context of ongoing commitment by the law school to advancing education in the lawyers' intellectual and ethical responsibilities'.[40] Presumably a history of law analysis cannot but take account of the particular economic arrangements and other societal structures in particular historical contexts.[41]

The central insight of post-structural theory that all knowledge is constructed and that knowledge and power are symbiotic has spawned a new kind of analysis of the law. In

---

38. Stewart Macaulay, "Law Schools and the World Outside Their Doors", 32 Journal of Legal Education, 1982, p. 506.
39. Arthur Leff, "Law and. . .", 87(5) Yale Law Journal, 1978, p. 989.
40. David Richards, "Liberal Political Cultural and the Marginalized Voice: Interpretive Responsibility and the American Law School", 45 Stanford Law Review, 1993, p. 1955 at p. 1978.
41. G. Edward White, "Reflections on the 'Republican Revival': Interdisciplinary Scholarship In the Legal Academy", 6 Yale Journal of Law and the Humanities, 1994, p. 1.

order to understand what is radical about the post-structural analysis it must be placed in the context of earlier analyses in the tradition of. law and economics or law and something else. For example, Marxist analysis of bourgeoisie law explains the rise of Liberal law as a response to the demands of an economic system changing from feudalism to capitalism. Since Marxism treats the economic system as the most important it does not have to pay much attention to the issues of bureaucratization of the state. Weber, on the other hand, being a sociologist can explain the rise of modern law in non-economic terms. Both analyses are concerned with explaining the same phenomenon, i.e. the rise of modern law, which is supposed to be rational, universal, principled. Yet their explanations focus on one or the other aspect of law defined as relevant by the particular conventions of their discipline.[42]

Post structural analysis could better integrate various aspects of law and society as it acknowledges the social construction of knowledge and the link between knowledge and power. True interdisciplinarity would also be achievable as post-structural theory undermines the enterprise of building meta-theories which are invariably developed within the bounds of separate disciplines. Post-structuralism could be especially useful in re-conceptualizing legal education as it could help in examining how the law has built notions of (narrow) valid legal knowledge.[43] This inquiry would in turn

---

42. For a Comparison between the views of Marx and Weber, see M.C. Western and J.S. Western, "Class and Inequality: Theory and Research", in J.M. Najman and J.S. Western (eds.), A Sociology of Australian Society: Introductory Readings, Macmillan, Melbourne, 1988.

43. For example see Susan Stewart, Crimes of Writing: Problems in the Containment of Representation, Duke University Press, Durham, London, 1994 for the argument that law is a form of writing yet it manages to deflect attention from its susceptibility to interpretation and its temporality. For examples of feminist legal post-structural analyses see Lisa D. Brush, "The Curious Courtship of Feminist Jurisprudence and Feminist State Theory", 19 Law and Social Inquiry, 1994, p. 1059; Drucilla Cornell, Transformations: Recollective Imagination and Sexual Difference, Routledge. 1993, pp. 1-11 and 112-94; Roger Berkowitz, "Risk of the Self" book review, 9 Berkeley Women's Law Journal, 1994, p. 175.

lead to an examination of the ways to make legal knowledge truly inclusive, able to take into account all relevant perspectives/standpoints.

Professional *versus* Academic Legal Education

It is commonplace in debates about the content and scope of legal education to come across the dichotomy between the needs of the professional and academic expectations. Put simply, legal education appropriate for future practitioners is supposed to be different from legal education for academics and other non-profession related jobs of policy-makers, community workers, etc. I disagree with this conceptualization of the issue for it shows a fundamental lack of understanding of the post-structural theorists' claim that all knowledge is crucial to maintaining privileges and hierarchies. I wish to argue that legal knowledge is justified as natural, neutral, universal, etc. by relying on conceptual tools like the public and private distinction or a particular understanding of freedom. Deconstruction of these concepts and definitions allows us to see the link between those who define these concepts and their positions of privilege maintained by such explanations. When feminist post-structuralists argue that all knowledge is biased or comes from some perspective it is a claim applicable to all aspects of law of the practitioners and of the academics and non-practitioners. It is important to understand that the narrow boundaries of legal knowledge in procedural rules, evidentiary rules, adequate proof, etc. all go into creating a narrow definition of legal doctrine-in turn considered the only valid concern of lawyers be they judges. solicitors. barristers or law students and academics.[44] But if law is to be something more than a legitimator of *status quo* it must be important for the members of the profession as well as the academics at least to inculcate habits of self-reflectivity in the

44. Twinnings says that a survey conducted in Britain showed that the profession found the law students inadequate as they were unable to construct or analyse arguments. William Twinning *supra* n. 26 at p. 184.

construction of legal knowledge. A lawyer arguing on a technicality in the court and getting an acquittal for her/his client who may be guilty is as implicated in the process as a law teacher taking a position that law is a means of oppression therefore it ought to be ignored or trashed. The claims of the objectivity of law and its personal nature are the specific means used to absolve individuals from taking any responsibility for the consequences of their views. But if it could be accepted that legal knowledge, like any other knowledge, is constructed continuously it would become that much more possible to show agency and therefore responsibility for creating ethical legal rules and system.

I will use two examples to illustrate this point. The first example is from the Australian family law. The Family Law Act, 1975 is a Commonwealth legislation and it governs the dissolution of any marriage in Australia. One of the distinctive features of the Family Law Act is supposed to be the discretion given to the Family Court to decide the custody/access issues relating to the children (the terminology has recently changed to care and control). This discretion is to be exercised solely in the best interests of the child. One of the well known judgments under the Family Law Act, in the Marriage of Gronow and Gronow,[45] involved a custody dispute between the mother and the father. The father was a medical doctor and the mother was a full dine nurse. There was not much to distinguish between the mother and the father as the more desirable custodial parent. The decision turned on whether it was preferable to leave a young child with the mother and whether the Australian family law recognized the mother preference principle. The court said, among other things, that even if a principle of mother as the preferred custodial parent for a young child had operated in the past it was no longer appropriate to continue with it. The societal conditions had changed and nowadays mothers and fathers were changing their parenting patterns and both were getting involved in looking after children as well as working outside the home. The father was given custody of the child.

45. 1979 (144) CLR 513.

The point I wish to make is that the judges are given discretion under the law but this discretion is exercised by them in the context of what they 'know'. A judge in common law systems is not expected to be well versed in social sciences or feminist analyses. Thus when, they come to an issue of parenting patterns they will invariably rely on their common-sense knowledge, derived from their social acquaintances. If these judges had been expected to understand and apply feminist analyses of the position of women in contemporary societies, the notions of femininity, ideas of proper gender roles, restricted economic independence of most women, etc., they may have been less complacent in accepting that parenting patterns in our society have changed that much. There is enough evidence available to demonstrate that women are the overwhelming majority of primary parents and that a direct consequence of such responsibilities is that women are economically disadvantaged.[46] If such knowledge was made part of the valid sources of information for judges and other legal functionaries the legal discourse about parenting would be more reflective of actual conditions existing in society rather than the imagined world views of the privileged in society. Moreover, the incorporation of ideas in legal discourse has an inevitable effect in shaping our understanding of 'reality' and it is obviously important that law should encompass a broad base.

The same point is well illustrated by a recent judgment in India's criminal law. In *Bhanwari Devi's case*[47] the magistrate acquitted the defendants of the charges of gang rape of Bhanwari Devi. The details of the judgment make for

---

46. Peter McDonald, The Economic consequences of Marriage Breakdown, Australian Institute of Family Studies, Melbourne, 1985; Lenore Wietzman, The Divorce Revolution: The Unexception Social and Economic Consequences for Women and Children in America, Free Press, New York, 1985.

47. I have relied on the English translation of the judgment of District and Sessions Court in the case State *v.* Ramkaran (The Bhanwari Devi Gang Rape Case) delivered on 15-11-1995 in Jaipur. This translation was very kindly supplied to me by Professor B.B. Pande, Law Faculty, Delhi University.

numbing reading. The magistrate in his full authority decided to interpret the gang rape of a married woman as culturally implausible, that is the respected male members of society, of varying ages, and of different castes, were unlikely to have engaged in sexual intercourse with a woman in the presence of others. The crucial point here is that the magistrate is not expected to be informed of gender issues, power imbalances between the gang rapists and the victim, extensive literature on rape as a means of exercising sexual power over women or the notions of chastity for women which make a rape victim the culprit. If the magistrate is not even aware of these ideas there is not much hope that he can be sensitive to the power imbalances at play or be sympathetic to the victim but the rub lies in that he is not expected to. He is free to rely on his understanding of the Indian society and according to him Indian culture has not fallen to this extent that respectable men would engage in gang rape. This outcome is the function of a narrow conception of legal knowledge and for that reason the suggestion that the judiciary needs to reeducated is entirely inappropriate.

In Australia and some other first world countries there is robust debate happening about the need to re-educate the judges and make them more sensitive to the concerns raised by feminists, race theorists and minority community members.[48] In response the opponents of such moves decry the efforts to taint the neutrality and universality of law with inappropriate ideas. I wish to argue that re-education of the judiciary will not be of any use as long as feminist analyses of law are presented as bits of radical or progressive ideas not really relevant to legal knowledge. The most that could be expected from re-educating the judges is that some of them will have the goodwill to take on board new ideas but

48. See for example, Senate (Senate Standing Committee on Legal and Constitutional Affairs) Gender Bias and the Judiciary, 1994; Access to Justice Advisory Committee, Access to Justice—An Action Plan, Commonwealth of Australia, 1994; Ruth Phegan, "Judicial Education: A Mechanism of Avoidance", 5 Polemic, 1994, p. 79; Kathy Mack, "Gender Bias and Judicial Education", Law Society of the ACT Gazette, February 1995, p. 40.

it will be a personal choice and it has nothing to do with the nature of law as such. It is important to emphasize that what is at stake is a radical reconceptualization of legal knowledge. Secondly, the academy is the place for such reflection and development of ideas. A radically restructured legal education is the only way of realistically achieving such a transformation.

CONTENT AND METHODOLOGY OF LEGAL EDUCATION

In the literature on education there is widespread agreement that in any discipline the educationists must clearly articulate the aims of education, the means of achieving such aims, and have clear conceptions of student learning and good teaching.

It is undeniable that it is time for Indian educationists to take the task of legal education seriously and examine the presuppositions on which most legal education is structured.[49] I wish to argue that the legal feminist ideas can assist in widening the scope of legal education and making it a meaningful experience for everyone. Both the content and methodology must be reformulated with the fundamental aim of enabling the students to critique legal knowledge and learn to take responsibility for construction and legitimation of ideas about the law. This view however, is a reversal of much conventional knowledge that the practitioners including the judges are the real custodians of the law but it has a reason for its emphasis. The reason I am emphasizing the role of legal education in such reconceptualization is that the task of analyzing the nature of knowledge is best suited to the capabilities of the academics and scholars of law-activities carried out in the universities.

Secondly, even if the influence of educators is severely limited it is nevertheless the responsibility of educators to

49. The task to be successful has to be holistic. Aspects of legal education are sporadically critiqued but I suggest it needs to be done systematically and the focus must move beyond the curriculum and include teaching methodology as well as assessment schemes. See for example Rajeev Dhavan *supra* n. 33.

strike for making ethics and morals an integral part of legal education. This requires a more imaginative response than simply offering a course on legal ethics. Deborah Rhode says that "Most recent psychological research indicates that well-designed curricula can significantly improve capacities for moral reasoning and that moral judgment bears some modest relationship to moral behaviour."[50] If faculty members decline to discuss ethical matters as they arise in each substantive area they encourage the future practitioners to do the same.[51] Moreover as Chickering and Reisser argue: "Institution that emphasize intellectual development to the exclusion of other strengths and skills reinforce society's tendency to see some aspects of its citizens and not others. Just as individuals are not just consumers, competitors, and taxpayers, so students are not just degree seekers and test takers. To develop all the gifts of human potential, we need to be able to see them whole and to believe in their essential worth."[52]

For a start the content of legal education must move beyond its exclusive focus on legal doctrine. The aim of legal education must be to generate self reflective and critical capacities of students.[53] A fundamental requirement for this is to challenge the neutrality and universality claims of the law by analysing the conceptual tools used in such reasoning. Feminist post-structural theories can help in exploring the ways in which boundaries around what is defined as valid

---

50. Deborah Rhode, "Missing Questions: Feminist Perspective on Legal Education." 45 Stanford Law Review, 1993, p. 1547 at p. 1562. She cites, among others. James S. Leming, 'Curricular Effectiveness in Moral/Values Education: A Review of Research', 10 Journal of Moral Education, 1981, p. 147; James R. Rest, Moral Development: Advances in Research and Theory, Praeger, New York. 1986. See also Harry T. Edwards, "The Growing Disjunction between Legal Education and Legal Profession", 91 Michigan Law Review, 1992, p. 34 for the argument that students need ethical training.

51. *Ibid.*

52. Arthur W. Chickering and Linda Reisser, Education and Identity, Jossey-Bass Publishers, San Francisco, 1993, p. 41.

53. See for example, D. Schon, Educating the Reflective Practitioner: Towards a New Design for Teaching and Learning in the Professions, Jossey-Bass, San Francisco, 1987.

knowledge are constructed. Gender as an analytical concept can be utilized to examine the processes of constructing legal ideas within the mainstream well as within feminist discourses. As a consequence the interdependence of law, state and society would become an integral part of legal analyses.

As it would no longer be appropriate to have an exclusive emphasis on the judgments of the courts the methodology of legal education would also have to be reconceptualized. I will focus on the following issues, but they are only some of the issues that need attention: theories of student learning, pedagogical tools, generation of authoritarian or cooperative modes of education.

Teaching *versus* Learning

It is my argument that the primary object of legal education is to develop the critical abilities of the students, to sensitize them to the assumptions on which the literature (legal or non-legal) is based. Enabling the students to examine the basis of any argument can help in changing the ways in which students understand, experience and conceptualize the world.[54] In pursuing this aim the idea is definitely not to indoctrinate students to adopt a particular view but to make it possible that students learn to formulate their own views.

According to Ramsden[55] learning is a change in understanding, a qualitative change in a person's view of reality. Understanding in turn is the way in which students apprehend or discern phenomena related to the subject. It is not to be confused with what they know about them or how they can manipulate them. A substantial part of higher education literature focuses on the students and it is widely accepted that the objective of education or teaching should be to facilitate learning.[56]

---

54. Paul Ramsden, Learning to Teach in Higher Education, Routledge, London, 1992, p. 4.
55. *Ibid.*
56. Noel Entwistle & Paul Ramsden, Understanding Student Learning, Croom Helm Ltd., London, 1983.

The single most important feature of the literature on student learning is that the student is considered to be the active agent and Ramsden[57] argues that learning is best conceptualized as a relation between a person and a phenomenon, that is the way in which anyone goes about learning is a relation between the person and the material being learned. The concept of approach to learning draws intention to the qualitative aspect of learning—the what and how of learning rather than how much. In the literature on approaches to learning it is well accepted that there are two broad categories of deep and surface learning. Entwistle[58] says that the most salient correlates of approaches to learning are the contrasting forms of motivation-intrinsic motivation (learning out of interest) facilitates deep and organized learning; extrinsic motivation (learning geared to vocational qualification) compels reliance on surface approach. Marton and Saljo[59] however, argue that it is important to make an analytical separation between the referential (what) aspect behind the deep/surface and the organizational (how) aspect of the holistic/surface dichotomies. Only when they are identified separately can the relationship between them be demonstrated, i.e. certain meaning orientation leads to a certain way of organizing the text and parts of it and the way of organizing the text leads to a certain referential meaning being abstracted from it.

Ramsden[60] argues that both deep and surface learning

---

57. *Supra* note 54 at p. 40.
58. Entwistle has sought to operationalise and investigate the correlates of deep and surface approaches to learning with the operation and comprehension learning styles. He has designed the ASI inventory to assess 16 sub-scales across four domains and according to him this inventory has produced four main factors: deep, surface, organised and strategic. Noel Entwistle, "A Model of the Teaching-Learning Process", in John Richardson, M. Eysneck, and D.W. Piper (eds.). Student Learning: Research in Education and Cognitive Psychology, Milton Keynes, Philadelphia, 1987, pp. 13-28.
59. Ference Marton and Roger Saljo, "Approaches to Learning", in F. Marton, D. Hounsell and N. Entwistle (eds.), The Experience of Learning, Scottish Academic Press, Edinburgh, 1984, pp. 36-55 at p. 44.
60. *Id.* at p. 44.

are approaches to learning. Approaches to learning are not something students have but represent what the learning task is for a student. In changing the approaches to learning one is not changing the student but the aim is to change the students' experiences, perceptions or conceptions of something. Marton and Saljo[61] accept that deep/holistic approach is not always the best approach but say that it is the best or only way to understand learning materials. However, what is deep or surface approach is supposed to be different for each discipline. I wish to pursue this idea for the discipline of Law because I am interested in encouraging deep learning in Law students and for that I must first examine what may constitute deep learning in the discipline of law. Subsequently I will examine the question whether students can be encouraged to adopt a deep approach to learning. All these issues have a direct correlation to the design of the curriculum, the assessment schemes and the methods of teaching.

As discussed above a major challenge to the narrow focus of legal education has been presented by the critical legal studies, feminists and other interdisciplinary movements. To recapitulate very briefly, these critiques in various forms challenge the claim that law is autonomous, objective, neutral or principled. In addition to critiquing the doctrine there is lively interest in interdisciplinary study of law. This is now being done as a law centred exercise rather than making law an aspect of the study of sociology or anthropology or any other discipline. At least one upshot of these critiques is that there is renewed debate about the aims of legal education. No longer is it possible for any school of thought to be smug about the aims or content of legal education. Therefore, at the very least it is problematic to define what may constitute deep approach to learning in law.

I am interested in feminist analyses of law. However, it is not merely a personal preference but my emphatic assertion that feminist analyses can deconstruct claims about neutrality, objectivity and universality of law. It is important

61. *Id.* at p. 46. 107

to challenge the conventional knowledge about law in order to expose students to the constructed nature of all knowledge. If the aim is to make it possible for students to take responsibility for the views they hold and defend their choices as conducive to creating a just social system a first step must be to enable them to cross boundaries.[62] Such an education will be a transformative enterprise in that students will see how they, and everyone else, is implicated in creating knowledge and justifying or changing social relations. Thus deep learning in Law has to be about understanding one's responsibility in the construction of legal knowledge. If this view of deep learning is accepted I believe students can be motivated to adopt this approach to learning. This is especially so if the changed content of legal education is supplemented with appropriate methodology of teaching.

One of the fundamental contributions of feminist thought is to stress that learning environments should be less competitive and more collaborative, not only for women students but for everyone.[63] For example, Susan Williams argues that the Socratic method is completely compatible with feminist epistemology. But for that the need is to revive the ideal of Socratic dialogue, in which knowledge and challenges to knowledge flow in both directions. However, the questions should seek to engage both rational and emotional responses like empathy and moral outrage because knowledge creation occurs through all these capacities.[64]

I believe that feminist emphasis on cooperative learning is another way of describing what is termed collaborative learning in education literature. Kenneth Bruflee[65] explains the

---

62. Henry A Giroux, Border Crossings Cultural Workers and the Politics of Education, Routledge, New York, 1992; Bell Hooks, Teaching to Transgress: Education as a Practice of Freedom, Routledge, New York, 1994.
63. Margo Culley and Catherine Portuguese (eds.), Gendered Subjects: The Dynamics of Feminist Teaching, Routledge Kegan Paul, Boston, 1985.
64. Susan Williams, "Legal Education, Feminist Epistemology and the Socratic Method", 45 Suinford Law Review, 1993, p. 571.
65. Kenneth A. Bruffee, "Learning and the Conversarion of Mankind", in Anne S. Goodsell, Michelle R. Maher, Vincent Tinto, Barbara

meaning of collaborative learning as learning takes place when students engage in conversation with each other and with the teacher about the subject-matter of their discipline. He bases his argument on the view that conversation and thought are causally related. Rather than assuming thought to be an essential attribute of the human mind it must be understood as an artefact created by social interaction. We think because we can talk, and the ways in which we think are dependent on how we have learnt to talk. If students can learn to converse with each other it would become possible for them to understand how all knowledge is justified social belief, maintained by the 'normal discourse' of communities of knowledgeable peers.[66] A community of knowledgeable peers is a group of people who accept the same paradigm, the same code of values and assumptions. They agree upon the set of conventions about what counts as a relevant contribution, relevant question, good argument or good criticism. Thus, collaborative learning allows students to take part in what is going rather than assimilate a given truth. Significantly Bruffee goes on to argue that it is the task of teachers to demonstrate the provincial nature of normal discourse and thus enable students to transgress the conventions of their disciplines and engage in 'abnormal discourse'. It is this possibility for generating new knowledge that makes education a transformative exercise.

It follows that a legal education aiming to empower students and the teachers to be responsible actors would have to abandon large lecture rooms and design teaching environments where genuine interaction between people is possible. There is considerable literature available discussing legal feminist teachers' efforts to generate such cooperative environments.[67]

Smith, and Jean McGregor (eds.)., Collaborative Learning: A Sourcebook for Higher Education, National Centre on Post-secondary Teaching, Learning and Assessment (NCTLA), Pennsylvania State University, Pennsylvania, 1992, pp. 23-33. The following discussion is based on this article.

66. *Id.* at p. 26. For this point Bruffee cites Richard Rorty, Philosophy and the Mirror of Nature, Blackwell, Oxford, 1979.

67. See for example, Mary Jane Mosman, "Otherness and the Law

FEMINIST LEGAL THEORY AS A FOUNDATION COURSE IN JURISPRUDENCE

A course in Feminist Jurisprudence is meant to serve as an introduction to some of the contemporary debates about the relationship between Law and Society. The debates in feminist jurisprudence have come a long way since the days of describing this topic as 'Women and the Law' or other similar characterizations which suggested that all that we needed to do was to accommodate some 'women-related demands'. The readings in the following sections will make it obvious that feminist critiques of law and jurisprudence amount to a comprehensive critique of the very assumptions on which such theorization is premised. It follows therefore, that Feminist Jurisprudence is not a special interest project which some of us have the option or the opportunity to engage with. Instead this course is designed to demonstrate that a comprehensive understanding of jurisprudence demands a competent understanding of feminist jurisprudence or legal theory.

Structure and Methodology

The course can be structured around a set of interrelated topics and readings. The readings are organized under separate headings but by their very nature they do not form discrete or self-contained sections. The basic aim is to show the interconnections between different ideas and their manifestations in different views of the law. The subject area of Feminist Legal Theory is a very dynamic area and there is a tremendous amount of interesting literature available. However, since we can only fit in a limited amount of readings a somewhat arbitrary choice will be made. The

School: A Comment on Teaching Gender Equality", I Canadian Journal of Women and Law, 1985, p. 213; Martha Fineman, "Theory in Law: The Difference it Makes", 2 Columbia Journal of Gender and Law, 1992, p. 1; Patricia Cain, "Teaching Feminist Legal Theory at Texas", 38 Journal of Legal Education, 1988, p. 165: Morrison Torrey, Jackie Casey and Karin Olson, "Teaching Law in a Feminist Manner", 13 Havard Women's Law Journal, 1990, p. 87.

articles are selected for their readability, strength of argument and based on the consideration whether they represent a well known perspective in the area.

Assessment Scheme[68]

Preferably each student will be expected to write two essays, one to be handed in the mid-term and one at the end of the term. The second essay will be a research essay where each student will choose their own topic for research. The rationale for not choosing exams is that students should not feel compelled to memorize the reading materials. By expecting them to write essays, hopefully we can enable them to develop their skills for critiquing and building their own arguments. It is a non-authoritarian view of education and it puts the responsibility for learning on the students—as they have no compulsion to study for exams. The topics for two essays in turn have different educational rationales. A set topic for the first essay is designed to test the students' understanding of the basic concepts employed in the literature. As a mid-term assignment it enables continuous assessment so that the students can be guided about their style and content of arguments. Feedback from the teacher at this stage will primarily serve a formative function. The second essay, at the end of the course, is designed as a research essay. It is aimed at generating skills for defining a research topic and managing the task of finding relevant literature, analysing the debates as well as substantiating a coherent argument.

Topic One: Why Jurisprudence?

The traditional meaning of Jurisprudence is that it is the science of Law. In order to understand the nature of Law various theorists have put forward arguments about the sources of authority of Law. In asking the question 'why do we accept the authority of law' there is an assumption that

68. It will of course have to be determined in consultation with the Head of School, other faculty members and the students of the particular institution.

fundamentally we are free human beings and any restraint on that freedom must be justified. Ideas about what does it mean to be an autonomous individual and who may restrict this autonomy on what basis, have undergone many developments over the ages. The change from feudalism to industrial society, especially in Europe, saw the rise of new ideas about individual autonomy, legitimacy of the modern state and the conception of Law. Even though these are European developments they have a crucial significance for us in order to understand the status of Law in contemporary India as they explain the origins of ideas in other cultures with their specific histories. It is only when we see the origins in their specific socio-historical context that we can start asking how suitable are these ideas for everyone. Yet it is also a fact that we in third world countries have to work with ideas about law which are a legacy of the colonial past of our country.

Topic Two: Liberalism as the philosophy of enlightenment

Conception of freedom or liberty in much of western political theory is as freedom from the state. Liberalism institutionalized this conception through the public/private distinction. The concepts of Public and Private are used to rationalize the limited scope of legal regulation. There are many critiques of Liberal conception of freedom as it excluded from its scope the non-propertied males, colonized peoples and women. For Indian law students it is especially relevant to examine how the British Liberal thinkers could simultaneously argue for equality and freedom and justify colonialism.

Topic Three: Extension of liberal principles to the excluded

- Women and Equality: Women in western democracies were the first to argue for extension of Liberal principles to them in the name of equality. However, the early feminists did not feel obliged to extend the principle of equality to non-white women, either in their own countries or in the colonized societies. In Indian universities the discourse on equality would necessarily include a critique of Liberalism and early western feminism.

Topic Four: Liberal feminism's promise whether misguided

Critique and defence of Liberalism: The early faith in Liberalism has been revised by feminists amongst others. As a consequence within feminist theory there is a robust discussion on different conceptions of equality. Although a lot of this literature is related to women in first world polities it lends itself to other uses. In the Indian context different conceptions of equality are directly relevant in dębates about personal laws. Whether different religions have their own conceptions of sex equality or even equality on the basis of religion is a topic of immense importance. It is crucial that Indian law students are equipped to develop these debates intelligently.

Topic Five: Legitimacy of the Stale and the rule of law

Liberal State and the idea of Rule of Law go hand in hand. However, in order to understand the connection the students must have an adequate understanding of the theories of the state. The assumptions underlying Liberal, Marxist and Feminist ideas about state must first be articulated and only then can students be expected to critique them. This is something that does not happen very often in law classes. It is a good illustration of the need to include study materials beyond legal literature. A good grasp of these issues will equip the students to discuss why the state can be expected to make appropriate Law Reforms. It in turn ties up with the debates about all kinds of social reform laws.

Topic Six: Relevance of gender to jurisprudence

The critiques of Liberal ideas of equality and the rule of law can next be developed in conjunction with feminist analyses and examine whether the norms and concepts used in various theories are gender neutral. An examination of the relevance of gender as an analytical concept will lay the foundation for examining the exclusionary devices used by all theories, including feminism. It will enable the students to question the constructed nature of all knowledge.

Topic Seven: Sameness/difference debate and essentialism in feminism

These debates allow ample opportunity to examine

whether neutral or unbiased knowledge can be created. It is specific mostly to the North American context but provides a good starting point for Indian law students to examine just about every aspect of the Indian legal system. The assumptions on which most of the Indian legal system operates are archaic to say the least. What is the logic for a country to continue with colonial institutions and principles of law should be one of the basic issues discussed in Indian law schools.

Topic Eight: Legal feminism and race: an example of feminisms' ability to accommodate differences

Once again the literature on this topic is specifically North American but it yields valuable ideas for Indian law students to apply and develop in their context. Indian society is pluralistic yet in Indian legal scholarship there is next to no discussion about the law's capacity to accommodate differences. The area of religious personal laws is treated as an exception to the rule rather than as a springboard for developing ideas about a truly just legal system in a pluralistic society.

Topic Nine: Recent critiques of liberal law

Critical Legal Studies are the supposedly radical critiques of Liberal-positivist theory of law. However, feminists have critiqued the CLS writers for their inability to make their analyses gender and race sensitive. In other words, just because a theory is radical does not guarantee that it will also aspire to social justice. Ideas about law reform and legal analysis generally must respond to these critiques. The particular significance of this issue for Indian legal education is that it can enable the students and academics to develop legal analyses which are in tune with the prevailing social conditions in India rather than constantly work with ideas developed in very different contexts.

Topic Ten: Post modernism or post-structuralism and deconstruction

The contemporary developments in legal theory as in most other disciplines are often described by one of the above labels. For Indian legal thinkers it is important to understand the reasons for these shifts in modes of thinking and then decide whether the critiques have any use for them. The post-modern turn in western thought has been described as a paradigm shift. It is happening in the context of increasing globalisation. And for that reason alone it cannot be ignored by Indian thinkers. However, what is required is a serious engagement with this development rather than unthought through application.

Topic Eleven: Post-modernism in feminist legal theory

Feminist legal theory has adopted post-structural ideas and to that extent is a useful extension of these new developments. It is useful because feminists have tried to realize the social justice potential of post-structural thought. In the Indian context these ideas can be further developed to create analyses of contemporary laws and develop alternatives.

Topic Twelve: Feminist theory and legal education

I believe that towards the end of this course the students can be expected to respond to the education philosophy which permeates the design of this course. It will allow the students to decide whether in their view the study of law could still he organized in a narrow manner. The purpose of this discussion would be to articulate the connections between education and society. The law students who are educated in this manner will most likely carry a different conception of their roles once they have finished at the University.

Topic Thirteen: Some contemporary debates in feminisms

Readings in post-colonialism and feminism will enable the students to read and critique the latest writings in feminism.

At the end of the course the students would be asked to choose any area of interest to them and analyse it in the light of the ideas present in this course. For example, it would be very topical to define a topic as: Uniform Civil Code—A Case Study? Hopefully the students would be in a position to write an essay on Uniform Civil Code that goes beyond the standard formulations of religious rights versus gender equality or minority *versus* majority rights. It would be a definite advance in the debate if the students could at least begin to formulate ideas about a feminist argument for a Uniform Civil Code.

Appendix

Topic One

(i) Introduction

J.C. Smith, 'The Unique Nature of the Concepts of Western Law', in Csaba Varga (ed.) Comparative Legal Cultures, Dartmouth, 1992.

J.M. Kelly, A Short History of Western Legal Theory, Chapter 6, Clarendon University Press, 1992.

(ii) Rise of the Modern State

Gianfranco Poggi, The Stale, Its Nature, Development and Prospects, Chapters 3 and 4, Stanford University Press, 1990.

Topic Two

Paternalism versus Democratism-debate between Locke and Filmer

Linda Nicholson, Gender and History, Chapters, Columbia University Press, 1986.

Ross Poole, Morality and Modernity, Routledge, 1991, Chapters 2 and 3.

Genevive Lloyd, The Man of Reason, Routledge, 1984, Introduction and Chapter 5.

Carolc Pateman, "Feminist Critiques of the Public and Private", in A. Phillips (ed.), Feminism and Equality, Basil Blackwell, 1987.

Topic Three

Alison Jaggar, Living with Contradictions: Controversies in Feminist Social Ethics, 1994, pp. 1-12.

Mary Wolistonecraft, 'Vindication of the Rights of Women' excerpted in J. Cooper and S. Cooper (eds.), The Roots of American Feminist Thought, Allyn and Bacon Inc., 1973, pp. 15-50.

Susan Okin, 'John Stuart Mill: Liberal Feminist' in Women in Western Political Thought, Princeton University Press, 1979, pp. 197-232.

Anne Phillips, 'Women and Equality', in Phillips (ed.) Feminism and Equality, Basil Blackwell, 1987.

Topic Four

Critique of Liberalism

Nadine Taub and Schneider, 'Women's Subordination and the Law', in D. Kairys (ed.) The Politics of Law, Pantheon Books, 1982, pp. 117-39.

Zillah Eisenstien, The Radical Future of Liberal Feminism, Longman, 1981, pp. 3-11 and 33-54.

Fanny Tabak, 'Obstacles to Implementing Equal Rights in Third World countries', in Zenon Bankwoski and Neil MacCormick (eds.), Women's Rights and The Rights of Man, Aberdeen University Press, 1990, pp. 149-57.

Defence of Liberalism

Pauline Johnson, "Feminism and Liberalism", 14, Australian Feminist Studies, 1991, pp. 57-68.

Susan Wendell, "A Qualified Defence of Liberalism", 2(2), Hypatia, 1991, pp. 65-93.

Richard Parker, "The Rights of Man and the Goals of Women", in Zenon Bankwoski and Nell MacCormick (eds.), Women's Rights and the Rights of Maim, Aberdeen University Press, 1990, pp. 117-24.

Topic Five

(i) Liberal understanding of the rule of law

Bob Fryer *et al.* (eds.), Law, State and Society, Croom Helm, London, 1981, pp. 9-20.

Roger Cotterrell, The Sociology of Law: An Introduction, Butterworths, 2nd edn., 1994, pp. 72-73 and 92-103.

(ii) Marxist critiques

Piers Burns and R. Quinney (eds.), Marxism and the Law, John Wiley and Sons, 1982, pp. 181-83.

Shelley Gavigan, "Law, Gender and Ideology" in Anne Bayefsky (ed.), Legal Theory Meets Legal Practice, Canadian IVR, Edmonton, 1988, pp. 283-96.

(iii) State and law reform

Jeanne Gregory, "Sex Discrimination, Work and the Law", in B. Fine *et al.* (eds.).

Capitalism and the Rule of Law: From Deviancy Theory to Marxism, Hutchison of London, 1979, pp. 137-50.

D. Polan, 'Toward a Theory of Law and Patriarchy" in D. Kairys (ed.), The Politics of Law, Pantheon Books, 1982, pp. 294-303.

Catherine Mackinnon, Toward a Feminist Theory of the State, Harvard University Press, 1989, pp. 157-70.

Wendy Brown, "Finding the Man in the State", 18, Feminist Studies, 1992, pp. 7-34.

Topic Six

Relevance of gender in jurisprudence

Moira Gatens, "A Critique of the Sex/Gender Distinction", in Sneja Gunew (ed.), A Reader In Feminist Knowledge, Routledge, 1991, pp. 139-57.

Ross Poole, Feminine/Masculine and Representation, Allen and Unwin, 1990, pp. 48-61.

Carol Gilligan, In a Different Voice, Harvard University Press 1982, pp. 1-23, 128-74.

Nancy Holland, "The Opinions of Men and Women", Journal of Social Philosophy, 1993, pp. 65-80.

Robin West, "Jurisprudence and Gender", 55, The University of Chicago Law Review, 1988, pp. 1-72.

Topic Seven

Sameness/Difference debate and Essentialism in Feminism

Diana Fuss, Essentially Speaking, Routledge, 1989, pp. 1-21.

Arthur Brittan and Mary Maynard, Sexism, Racisms and Oppression, Basil Blackwell, 1984, pp. 180-205.

Joan Williams, "Deconstructing Gender", 87, Michigan Law Review, 1988-89, pp. 799-845.

Joan Scott, 'Deconstructing Equality *versus* Difference: Or The Uses of Post-structuralist Theory for Feminism", 14, Feminist Studies, 1988, pp. 33-50.

Topic Eight

Angela Harris, "Race and Essentialism in Feminist Legal Theory", 42, Stanford Law Review, 1990, pp. 581-616.

Martha Minow, "Beyond Universality", The University of Chicago Legal Forum, 1989, pp. 115-38.

Marlee Kline, "Race, Rack", and Feminist Legal Theory", 12, Harvard Women's Law Journal, 1989, pp. 115-50.

Trina Grillo, "Anti-Essentialism and Intersectionality", 10, Berkeley Women's Law Journal, 1995, pp. 16-30.

Topic Nine

James Boyle, Critical Legal Studies, Dartmouth, 1992, pp. i-liii.

Alan Hunt, The Critique of Law: What is critical about critical legal studies"? in P. Fitzpatrick and A. Hunt (eds.), Critical Legal Studies, Basil Blackwell, 1987, pp. 5-20.

Amy Bartholomew and A. Hunt, "Whats Wrong with Rights", 9, Law and Inequality, 1990, pp. 1-58.

Deborah Rhode, "Feminist Critical Theories", 42, Stanford Law Review, 1990, pp. 617-38

Carrie Menkel-Meadow, "Feminist Legal Theory, Critical Legal Studies, and Legal Education", 38, Journal of Legal Education, 1988, pp. 61-116.

Kathleen Lahey, "Women and Civil Liberties", in D. Leidholdt and J. Raymond (eds.), The Sexual Liberals and the Attack on Feminism, Pergamon Press, 1990, pp. 198-207.

Andrea Dworkin, "Women-Hating Right and Left", in D. Leidholdt and I. Raymond (eds.), The Sexual Liberals and the Attack on Feminism, Pergamon Press, 1990, pp. 28-40.

Patricia Williams, "Alchemical Notes: Reconstructing Ideals from Deconstructed Rights", 22, Harvard Civil Rights and Civil Liberties Law Review, 1987, pp. 401-447.

Sandra Harding, Whose Science? Whose Knowledge?: Thinking From Women's Lives, Open University Press, 1991, pp. 105-10.

Topic Ten

Margaret Davies, Asking the Law Question, The Law Book Co., 1994, pp. 219-76.

Mary Hawkesworth, "Knowers, Knowing and Known", in Malson *et al.* (eds.).

Feminist Theory in Practice and Process, University of Chicago Press, 1986, pp. 327-52.

Nancy Fraser and Linda Nicholson, "Social Criticism without Philosophy", in Linda Nicholson (ed.), Feminism/Post Modernism, Routledge, 1990, pp. 19-38.

Deborah King, "Multiple Jeopardy, Multiple Consciousness", Malson *et al.* (eds.), Feminist Theory in Practice amid Process, University of Chicago Press, 1986, pp. 75-106.

Topic Eleven

Clare Dalton, "Where We Stand", Berkeley Women's Law Journal, extracted in F. Olsen (ed.), Feminist Legal Theory, Dartmouth, 1995, pp. 1-15.

Susan Williams, "Feminist Legal Epistemology", 8, Berkeley Women's Law Journal, 1993, pp. 63-105.

Carol Smart, Feminism and the Power of Law, Routledge, 1989, pp. 4-25, and 138-65.

Lisa D. Brush, "The Curious Courtship of Feminist Jurisprudence and Feminist State Theory", 19, Law and Social Inquiry, 1994, pp. 1059-77.

Drucilla Cornell, Transformations: Recollective Imagination and Sexual Difference, Routledge, 1993, pp. 1-11 and 112-94.

Roger Berkowitz, "Risk of the Self" book review, 9, Berkeley Women's Law Journal, 1994, pp. 175-205.

Topic Twelve

Mary Jane Mosman, "Otherness and the Law School: A Comment on Teaching Gender Equality", 1, Canadian Journal of Women and Law, 1985, p. 213.

Martha Fineman, "Feminist Theory in Law: The Difference It Makes", 2, Columbia Journal of Gender and Law, 1992, pp. 1-18.

Patricia Cain, "Teaching Feminist Legal Theory at Texas", 38, Journal of Legal Education, 1988, pp. 165-81.

Morrison Torrey, Jackie Casey and Karin Olson, "Teaching Law in a Feminist Manner, 13, Harvard Women's Law Journal, 1990, pp. 87-135.

Topic Thirteen

Henry A. Giroux, "Post-Colonial Ruptures and Democratic Possibilities, Multiculturalism as Antiracist Pedagogy", 21, Cultural Critique, 1992, pp. 5-39.

Gayatri Spivak in Sarah Harasym (ed.), The Post-Colonial Critic: Interviews, Strategies, Dialogues, Routledge, 1990, pp. 67-74.

Kalpana Ram, "'Too Traditional' Once Again: Some Post-structuralists on the Aspirations of the Immigrant/ Third World Female Subject", 17, Australian Feminist Studies, 1993, pp. 5-28.

5

From Human Rights to the Right to be a Woman

UPENDRA BAXI

I

Mainstream feminist, human rights and social science scholarship (with a handful of eminent exceptions) does not seem overly concerned with this form of sub-continental violence against women,[1] describe it thus because sex

1. This is a revised version of a talk delivered (August 1997) under the auspices of the Gender Study Group, a group of student activists who inaugurated a discourse on gender violence and sexual harassment on the campus. The fact that I was occasionally their prime target for institutional critique during my term of office as the Vice-Chancellor of Delhi University was most welcome. So is the fact that activist students did endeavour to articulate a distinctive set of feminist concerns beyond the hurly-burly of campus-based party-oriented teacher and student union politics.

The editors of this volume and Dr. Ved Kumari made a number of suggestions concerning the scope of the early drafts of this essay. Their sense of unease has, I hope, enhanced the overall clarity of the final version.

Ms Pratiksha Baxi read the pre-final version, offering a number of insightful suggestions.

trafficking, like other forms of globalization, violates human rights across borders. There are no barriers to "free" movement of the objects for sexual service.[2] Indeed, when the Berlin wall fell it fell on the bodies of once proud socialist citizen-women and the inflow of some of these into the Indian industry is the standard urban male Indian conversational topic. This is a tragedy inviting sociology-of-knowledge type studies, which I do not explore here. But it remains true that the production of knowledge relevant to social action remains inadequate.

Further, we have very little understanding of the economics of these markets, class location of its managers and agents and complicity, active or passive, by political actors. Indeed, the analogy of market misleads somewhat: what has emerged in India is a nation-wide industry of systematic production for profit of women constructed as commodities. Yet few notable economic studies of sex trafficking are available. Nor are abundant sociological analyses of patterns of imposition of sexual slavery in terms of ethnicity or poverty. If law, policy and social action are ever to address seriously the question of regulation or elimination of this industry, knowledge has to assume a critical mass.

Again, the logics or 'paralogics' of human rights movements remain insufficient to translate into meaningful social reality any movement against sex trafficking. The existing human rights discourse has failed to address the politics of cruelty involved in sex trafficking. One does not have to construct any hierarchy of violation of women, or a hierarchy of suffering, to say that the present understanding of the category of violence against women does not quite entail any insightful grasp of endless organization of "rape for profit."[3] This raises uneasy interrogation concerning the process of engendering human rights.

---

2. Upendra Baxi and Lotika Sarkar *v.* State of Uttar Pradesh Writ Petition No. 1900 of 1981: (1983) 2 SCC 308; (1986) 4 SCC 106; (1998) 8 SCC 622; (1998) 9 SCC 388.
3. See Rape for Profit: Trafficking of Nepali Girls and Women to India Brothels, Human Rights Watch/Asia, New York, 1995.

Lastly, intractable problems confront narratives of victimage. There is an inherent passivity about the word 'victim' which denies to the violated all moral agency, the potential for everyday resistance in face of massive ongoing and flagrant violation of the self. Do we have archives of resistance by the victims of sex trafficking in India? No doubt, there remain available heroic narratives of 'elopement' from brothels, facilitated by a web of romantic love or organized acts of "rescue" and rehabilitation by social workers, occasionally mandated by courts even to the point of return to the country of origin. These are, no doubt, crucial oases in the deserts of non-understanding. But lying beyond these are narratives of constant combat with the practices of de-sexualization and everyday strategies of coping with a whole order of evils ingrained in a phallocentric civil society and a sado-masochistic state and law.

Equally important are movements of sex-workers. In Surat, in the early eighties, they engaged in the politics of naming: not calling themselves prostitutes or sex-workers they renamed themselves as roopjeevinis (wonder-workers of beauty) and staged a protest, appropriately at the statue of Mahatma Gandhi, against appropriation of their bodies as the 'perks' of office claimed by the police and even male "social workers." At last there now have emerged some associations of women sex-workers which articulate their own understanding of the human right to be, and to remain human, within the industry of sex trafficking.

Even at the best moment of human rights activism, women's suffering becomes commoditized, as my retelling of Kamla's story suggests. The problem of narrative integrity is here poignantly posed. To tell Kamla's story over and over again runs the risk of her becoming a perpetual narrate, a discursive object, a site of erudite knowledge practices. But not to tell her story also risks conscription into regimes of silence about the most pervasive form of human suffering. The very indictment of sensibility I make of human rights communities in India returns to haunt my own enterprise in this essay. And I know that being aware of the problematic of narrative integrity is by no means an answer to it. In any case, I now tell the story, the way it should be told, in order to revisit the vicissitudes of law, rights and justice.

II

Kamla's story is brutally simple. She was bought and sold from a state guest-house in Shivpuri, Madhya Pradesh three times in a week in 1981.

The third time she was bought was by three investigative journalists of the Indian Express, for an amount (Rs. 2500) which Justice Jamadar of the Bombay High Court was to describe in 1985 as being less than half the price of a a buffalo in the states of Punjab and Haryana.

There was a brief moment in the history of post-colonial India when rank and gross violation of Indian humanity was front-page news, a moment when the pre-globalizing Indian urban middle classes were still capable of being outraged and scandalized.

Arun Shourie, the then intrepid editor of the Indian Express was determined to judicialize the event: he asked me to help. He did a brief entitled"Why the Supreme Court Should Hear Us."[4] This needed doing as at that time social action litigation before the Supreme Court was still nascent (despite the initiation of Agra Women's Home case by Lotika Sarkar and myself[5]). And Arun's grasp of legal materials was indeed persuasive. He and I met Chief Justice Chandrachud in chambers; the learned Chief Justice was kind enough to inscribe the matter on the cause list of the Court. And a further happy development occurred: Soli Sorabjee, a constitutional jurist, agreed to appear for Kamla, a fortune seldom visited on hapless Indian women.

The Supreme Court promptly ordered that Kamla be placed in a Women's Home (Nari Niketan) in Delhi and ordered the Madhya Pradesh Government to account for the sordid state of affairs.

Before that could happen, Kamla disappeared, never to be traced. The Indian Express simply lost its nerve to pursue

4. See Arun Shourie, "On Why the Hon'ble Court Must Hear Us", (1981) 4 SCC (Jour) 1.

5. See *supra* n. 2 for a full citation: for a narrative of the case, see "Women in the Labyrinth of Law" in U. Baxi, Inhuman Wrongs and Human Rights, Har Anand, Delhi, 1994.

the matter and further through the adjudicatory process, despite my prodding Arun Shourie. No one knows. and no one has followed up, what happened to the investigation into Kamla's disappearance.

There the matter rests.
And so does Kamla.
But not wholly so.

She excited the imagination of Vijay Tendulkar, whose play by her name was staged 150 times and enacted in several Indian languages.

Not just this: Bollywood constructed a new wave movie called Kamla. Deepti Naval's portrayal of her was superb in the sense that she does not (like the heroic protagonists in new wave movies like Akhroash) speak a single word, signifying the total disarticulation, which the System imposes on her.

Where the playwright erred was in suggesting that the journalists failed in following up the story till its bitter human rights end. The error was even more outrageous in that the production violated the intellectual property rights of the Indian Express; for, didn't they own the narrative being of Kamla? The Express filed a suit in the Bombay High Court on the grounds of defamation (was there not something here, which even suggested to the lay mind that socially active journalists might have non-altruistic motives?). And then there was the violation of copyright owned by the corporate press (after all they owned the story).

The suit, on both counts, was rightly dismissed by the Bombay High Court.

III

We do not know where Kamla is, whether she is alive.

We do know, however, that hundreds of thousands of Kamlas (and not just in India) are being bought and sold in market overt, despite India's ratification of the Convention for the Elimination of Discrimination against Women (CEDAW), the programschrmft of the CEDAW and the effloresces of women's right movements in India and elsewhere.

How do we construct the meaning of these events?

One way is to look at the ways of commodification.

Kamla stands commodified in several ways.

First, she circulates as a commodity in the phallic markets of lecherous civil society and the state.

Second, she stands recommodified as an aesthetic event in the avant-garde markets: she makes possible a new genre of creative sensibility—whether named as "investigative journalism" or "new wave" theatre or movies or even public cause lawyering and judicial activism.

Third, she is recommoditized in the market of human rights and of judicial activism.

Fourth, she emerges, finally, as a high price-tag item in the intellectual property rights market, which now in a TRIPS-compliant India is more secure than it may have been in 1985.

Her manifold reproduction marks nuanced passages from the sphere of use-value into complex realms of exchange value. Her use-value (much less than the price of a buffalo in the State of Haryana, as the Bombay High Court estimated it) soars as exchange value in aesthetic, adjudicatory and now the new TRIPS markets.

Reproduced by different markets, her exchange value becomes many more times her use-value.

The constitutive markets bear a moment of reflection.

The original markets comprised filthy, lecherous swains whose moments of lust constitute the destiny of many a Kamla.

But in the realm of exchange value, the producers (like yourself and myself) are aesthetic beings, endowed with refined sensibilities to human sufferings and human rights, with precocious sensibility and self-images of a feminized world view and the solidarity of a transnational powerful sisterhood.

At their hands, the recommodification of Kamla, surely, entails no sublimation of phallocentric lust.

In fact, Kamla's recommodification is highly dialectical, isn't it? Is not her passage from the feudal markets of lust to the aesthetic human rights liberal markets an emancipatory transformation? Is not her progressive appropriation simultaneously a sign of her becoming, a mark of the coming liberation of all Kamlas?

IV

In what ways is Kamla's silence made to speak to us?

Obviously, she is rendered articulate through the mass media and the brief encounter with activist lawyering and judicial process. But for that recourse to happen, Kamla has to be bought, in violation of the criminal law. This primary purchase has, it may be argued, to be distinguished from a whole variety of subsequent appropriations by all those involved in the writing, producing and otherwise participating in the play and the movie (including audiences, reviewers) based upon her story. Not merely lawful, all these activities stand justified by a whole range of fundamental rights guaranteed by the Indian Constitution. But, it may be argued, the primary purchase stands "justified" by a benign intent, even if it did not result in a conscientious disobedience of the penal law. That benign intent aimed at the production of human rights results through an exposure of the intransigent evil. And a similar "justification" may also be advanced for all the secondary appropriations.

Such justifications represent the "utilitarianism" of rights argument which entail a restless calculus reflecting a constant readiness to interfere with rights in order to come out with a weighted minimum of rights-infringements."[6] But this is a complex calculus, requiring empirical substantiation. It is doubtful that the primary purchase by the Indian Express, and all subsequent appropriations of Kamla, did in effect produce that "weighted minimum of rights infringement." Do we really need, any hi-tech, capital-intensive empirical research to maintain that the several primary and associated purchases of Kamla achieved no such result?

---

6. Alan Gewirth, The Community of Rights, Chicago Press, Chicago. 1996, p. 51.

The Indian Express, as already noted, did not pursue Kamla's disappearance. Instead it allowed itself to be powerless against the veiled threats of criminal prosecution by the Madhya Pradesh Government ignoring the fact that the State was not moved by the slightest degree of prosecutorial vigour even by the fact that women were bought and sold from the state guesthouse! Nor did the Indian Express and the theatre or movie industry dedicate revenues from productions to combat flesh-markets. Nor, further, were the human sensibilities of the "aesthetic" consumers so violated as to inaugurate any national voice or campaign against this violation. Given this picture, the argument from utilitarianism of rights is not simply available.

In the result, the primary purchase (even if making Kamla audible, in miniscule ways) signifies only ways of her recommodification in the free speech markets summoning the force of the constitutional hagiographies of civil rights.

V

What human rights of Kamla were violated before the Supreme Court of India? When we ignore the fact of the "primary" purchase, it becomes possible to argue that her being bought and sold in market overt violated her right to life and liberty under Article 21 of the Indian Constitution (the stock-in-trade of Indian social action litigation). Her right to life, as it turned out, was further violated even as the judicial proceedings began, so long as we grasp the reality behind the sanitized term "disappearance."

With what human rights responsiveness did the Supreme Court of India 'deal' with these contentions? The answer is bleak: it never did. No judicial enquiry was initiated upon Kamla's "disappearance." No contempt proceedings ensued. Nothing happened at all.

It is scandalous that even when the petitioner initiative ebbed, judicial energies also waned. A few years down the road, the Supreme Court was to hold in Sheela Barse[7] that a

7. Sheela Barse *v.* Union of India (1988) 4 SCC 226: 1988 (2) SCALE 1574.

social action petition might be judicially nationalized. In other words, while denying a modicum of discursive dignity to a conscientious social action petitioner who withdraws in protest against the war of attrition waged against her by the State,[8] rights-protection casts a constitutional obligation on the Court to persevere, as it were, *suo moto*. No such consideration prevailed in Kamlas case.

Article 23, a fundamental right against exploitation, which specifically prohibits trafficking in human beings stood also clearly violated. The constitution-makers were so solicitous of this right that they went so far as to suspend Indian federalism (through Article 35) as to impose a constitutional duty on the Indian Parliament to make laws translating this right into a living social reality. The Court missed a valuable opportunity in mandating compliance with this obligation. This abdication in the face of enormous suffering of many a Kamla makes (despite all the wonderful things one says in celebration) Indian judicial creativity the lie of the land.

VI

When we ask: "Do women have a human right to immunity from being bought and sold as chattel in market overt?" The answer of contemporary Indian human rights community is in a resounding negative. The same community gets wholly incoherent when asked whether selling oneself or

---

8. It deserves to be recalled that Sheela Barse, a freelance journalist. had to face numerous adjournments because the Supreme Court rendered itself powerless even to compel state attorneys to file responsible affidavits in time. That meant that the petitioner had to invest her savings to fly into Delhi from Bombay and defray her own related expenses. Instead of fully grasping the anguish symbolised by her protest in withdrawing the petition, Justice Venkatachaliah (later Chief Justice of India, and now Chairperson of the National Human Rights Commission), reproached her in open court for her belligerence and transferred the matter to the Supreme Court Legal Aid Committee which simply did not march, as subsequent proceedings in the case, have amply demonstrated, the singular dedication of energies by Sheela Barse.

being sold by ones parents to sex trafficking as a mode of familial survival in dire economic circumstance is also violative of international human rights norms and standards?

This incoherence needs a fuller understanding. Human rights communities know full well that rights declarations or enunciations constitute only the first step in a (non-Concorde) journey of a thousand miles. But this become Hamlet—like on the second, third and fourth step.

Clearly, it is wrong for parents or relations to sell their daughters even as a way of cheating their way into bare survival. But does this pompous high middle-class morality require no more than high-minded ethical contempt for such conduct? Does it not impose upon them, aside from the self-assumed prerogative of passing severe moral judgments any "moral" or "ethical" requirement in terms of both the morality of duty and morality of aspiration? The morality of duty entails at least an obligation to understand and redress, as far as one can, situations of distress sales of girl children in market overt as well as obligations to rescue and rehabilitate those caught in this vicious web. The morality of aspiration demands as civic duty a serious concern with ways of promoting social and economic structures that attend to causes of distress and destitution, desexualisation and dehumanisation, pauperisation and powerlessness, anomie and alienation—all of which enable sex trafficking not merely to exist but to grow apace.

In the absence of such morally vibrant human rights cultures, declarations or enunciations of human rights norms and standards are, simply, dead on arrival. Protection and promotion of human rights is sensible only when human rights entail human responsibilities, not on the part of the abstract "We" but on all those specially favoured by fortune and therefore invested by history with an Opportunity to give voice to the violated and fostering collective capabilities to combat the very roots of structural violence in state and society. Can we expect the Indian State (or, indeed the world community of states) to take the human rights of many a Kamla seriously when even the most conspicuous of human and women's rights communities in India do neither appear, or in fact take seriously such violations?

For them, any recourse to languages of human rights enacts the cruel truth that the law and the state are not neutral sites of redressing injury but rather these "stand invested with the power to injure."[9] This truth is just a footnote on Friederich Nietzsche's trenchant interrogation of the state:

> State? What is that? Well then, open your
> ears to me, for now I shall speak to you
> about the death of peoples. State is
> the name of the coldest of all cold monsters.
> Coldly, it tells lies, too: lie grows out of its
> Mouth. "I, the state, am the people."[10]

Kamla embodies this truth. Surely, Kamla marks both the beginning and the end of social activist and judicial activism's flirtation with organised crime against women. The Lecherous Indian State and "civil" society are clearly beyond human rights redress, so entrenched are the vested interest formations benefiting from market overt in which women are bought and sold as chattel.

The invocation of constitutional/human rights of Kamla merely resulted in her "elimination." But the underlying relations of social production of her immiseration continue to flourish. And the mere assertion of human rights, regardless of the aesthetic of enunciation, simply does not help; in fact, it aggravates the injured selves.

VII

Perhaps, a part of the answer lies in the politics of human rights desire. In Kamla's case, it remains doubtful that this politics was marked by any consuming passion for the

---

9. Wendy Brown, States of Injury Power and Freedom in Late Modernity, Princeton University Press, Princeton, N.J., 1995.
10. The Portable Nietzsche, selected and translated, with an introduction, prefaces and notes, by 'Walter Kaufmann, Penguin Books, New York, 1976, p. 160.

protection and promotion of human rights of many a Kamla. Rather, it marked a peculiar moment of catharsis in the post-emergency India. In this moment the learned professions (journalists, lawyers and judges) felt the need to demonstrate that they, too, cared about the human rights of the Other India and not just for the political and civil rights of the Indian middle classes.[11]

Unsurprisingly, this 'class' which historically claims authorship of human rights and ownership of its languages, found itself utterly alienated from the subject positions and class location of Kamlas. The good faith affirmation of concern with the rights of the Other India having been made. The politics of human rights desire exhausted itself. There were no known ways by which this desire could further sustain itself, human rights praxis itself being an aspect of a deeply matriarchal class politics that cannot pursue in any sustained manner, the advocacy of the material interests of those violated. Surely, it is important to recall with Karl Marx[12], that the emancipatory logic of human rights is also at the same time a confessional statement concerning its limits. Granting the significance of this insight, we must also ask how does this ameliorate Kamlas of the world?

But it is equally crucial to remember that Marx himself acutely demonstrated that in certain historic moments these limits might be overcome[13]. How may this ever happen in the situation embodied by Kamla is the question here.

The situation is made all the more complex by the fact that sex trafficking markets are not just internal but subcontinental, and to some extent global. The severe cross-border dimensions of the market may not be addressed adequately by national legislation, policy and administration. The effete regional collaboration in South Asia in matters of

---

11. For an analysis of the four phases of the Emergency in India, and the resultant patterns of populist 'judicial' politics, see U. Baxi, The Indian Supreme Court and Politics, Eastern Book Company, Lucknow. 1979.
12. See U. Baxi, Marx, Law and Justice: Indian Perspectives, N.M. Tripathi, Bombay, 1993.
13. *Id.* at pp. 51-53.

cross-border collaboration in law enforcement makes any worthwhile amelioration unlikely, in the absence of major initiatives by concerned human and women's rights movements and activists. As far as I know, there has been no "feminization" of the agenda, in this respect, of the SARC (South Asian Regional Collaboration).

The fact that almost all South Asian states remain indifferent in their pursuit of "models of development", and now of "globalisation," makes official inadvertence understandable. After all, there remain more "important" issues to tackle in regional "collaboration" than the plight of women bought and sold in market overt, despite the international and constitutional pledges of, and for, human rights. But this makes the silence of human rights activists on this issue all the more deafening. In so far as this conspiracy of silence is maintained is there anything to choose for many a Kamla between the anti-activism of governments and states and the "activism" of the social, human rights activists?

VIII

When activism is thus bereft of an engagement, it becomes a human rights task to attend to voices of the violated. Access to this is not always easy amidst the cacophony of the established human rights classes.

I believe that the Indian Sex Workers' Manifesto marks a precious point of departure. It suggests that we locate the problem at the level of human rights enunciation itself, which is marked by the-male-in-the-state-and-the-law. This network assigns hegemony to the domain of politics of power (diplomatic exercises providing a fig-leaf to the "male-in-the-state" or recrudescent structures of patriarchy) and counter-power complicit human rights communities which thrive on the triumphalism of mere declaration of a human right norm and standard.

In contrast, the Manifesto speaks in the language of solidarity in struggle, not that of abstract enunciation of women's rights as human rights. What is necessary, according to the Manifesto, is to "challenge an all encompassing material and symbolic order." The "smallest of gains" lie, here and now, in creating "solidarity" and "collective strength" by the creation of a "positive identity" among those conscripted into sex trafficking.[14]

But the attainment of such solidarity has to occur, at the end of the Second Christian Century, through the manipulation of human rights markets. These entail a complex range of talents in what is, after all, becoming a high scramble for national and international resources, negotiating a relatively autonomous (of the funding agencies) agenda of action and the demands for legitimation with the beneficiaries as well as with the local and national state entailing a degree of corporatisation of NGO activity.

Added to all this is the task of successful commoditisation of human rights. This entails, on the one hand creation of networks of both investors and consumers for specific human rights and on the other, and related but distinct, the task of overcoming both human rights weariness and wariness[15]. Techniques of commoditisation are essential, especially to mobilise assault on compassion fatigue among diverse constituencies of human rights, especially the wider public which easily tires of having to cope with stories of so many human rights violations.[16]

It is relatively easy now to understand why the markets for human rights to combat those in trafficking in women are

---

14. See The Sex Workers' Manifesto, Mahila Samanwaya Committee, sexworknet @gn.apc.org (emphasis added.).

15. See Upendra Baxi, "Human Rights Education: the Promise of the Twenty-first Century?" in George J. Andreapoulos and Richard Pierre Claude (eds.), Human Rights Education for the Twenty-First Century, University of Pennsylvania, Pittsburgh, 1997, p. 142; For a full version, see http://www.pdhre.org.

16. See on this the most rewarding study of Amnesty's techniques of commoditisation of torture, cruel and inhuman and degrading punishment and treatment, Stanley Cohen, Denial and Acknowledgment : The Impact of Information About Human Rights Violations, Center for Human Rights, The Hebrew University of Jerusalem, 1995; see also, for further elaboration of the human rights market notion, Upendra Baxi, The Voices of Suffering and the Future of Human Rights", IOWA Journal of Transnational Law and Contemporary Problems, forthcoming.; and *Id.*, The Future of Human Rights, forthcoming, 1999.

so poorly organised. These have, by the end of the century, accomplished the naming of the evil and production of new moral languages. The first human rights instrument concerning women's rights was the Convention on Trafficking in Women, followed by the Supplementary Convention on the Abolition of Slavery, the State Trade and Institutions and Practices Similar to Slavery, the Convention Against Torture and other Cruel, Inhumane and Degrading Treatment or Punishment, and above all the Convention on the Elimination of All Forms of Discrimination Against Women [CEDAW]. Regional instruments and national constitutions and laws adapt the international human rights languages towards enhancement of implementation. But one has to look at concerned communities enunciations (for example, the Indian manifesto and the Draft Convention Against Sexual Exploitation[17]) to appreciate a very different mode of enunciation of human rights of women.

Overall, the normative triumph has been matched by comprehensive failure on the ground. It is this failure which, in a sense, tens of thousands of Kamlas interrogate. The contemporary ways of organisation and operation of markets for human rights of women have been a combined case of both marker and state failures. Is this so because the enunciative triumph itself has been deeply flawed? Or because the women's human rights movements are too heavily focused on the politics of identity/status rights? Or because the roots of organised markets of chattel slavery lie in policies of planned impoverishment which human rights languages can barely address? Many other possible reasons, including the lecherous character of political power, may also be added to this volume of interrogation.

Unless anguished introspection on these questions occurs in a sustained way (even as the world celebrates the Golden Jubilee of the Universal Declaration of Human Rights) markets for human rights will remain underdeveloped even in the first half of the next century.

---

17. See for a full text, Kathleen Bary, The Prostitution of Sexuality, New York University Press, New York, 1995.

IX

The Indian Sex-Workers' manifesto suggests that we locate the problem at the level of human rights enunciation itself. It suggests, to my mind, a paradigmatic shift from the languages of human rights to those of human solidarity. The former assign agency to the networks of hegemonic power that politics of human rights desire where it becomes increasingly difficult to disentangle politics of power (diplomatic exercises aimed at providing fig-leafs to the male-in-the-state) and that of counter-power (complicit human rights communities celebrating merely the enunciative triumphalism of human rights).

In contrast, the Manifesto's shift to languages of solidarity in suffering stresses the authorship of human rights to the communities of 'misfortune' through rhetorical devices in which "positive identity" is shaped by the moral agency of those who suffer, not by governments and NGOs who pursue their own politics of power and resistance.

The latter remain prisoners of their own categories: "rape", "sexual assault", "sex trafficking." The solidarity languages interrogate these categories. Sex-work comprises all these (on a continual time/space scale) and more. And the obligations of solidarity within suffering provide languages which remain relative strangers to the human rights discourse and practice.

The question they pose is very different: What is to be done? Done, in the interim, till that point of time when the utopia of elimination of markets which construct women as sexual 'objects', realises itself? It instead addresses the question: How may the solidarity of the oppressed transform the languages of human rights in ways through which these languages are no longer limits upon solidarity but become instead its vehicle? Put another way, it redirects attention to the question: what do you do in a situation of institutionalised rape to render the conveniently labelled communities of misfortune[18] into a community of human rights?

---

18. For this distinction between "misfortune" and "injustice", see Judith Shklar, The Faces of Injustice, Yale University Press, New Haven, 1991.

Of course, many 'strategies' may seem available if women's movements and human rights groups had the time to campaign. Even these may not address situations of elimination or liquidation of many a Kamla. But the second-best strategies include:

- Calls for rigorous implementation of the 1949 Convention.
- Invocation of Article 23(3) of the International Convention on Civil and Political Rights [avoiding fake marriages by traffickers] ensuring a human right to marriage with "the free and full consent of the intending spouses."
- Marshalling of the ILO Convention 29 [Article 2.1] Concerning Forced or Compulsory Labour [which must include forced sexual labour].
- Mobilizing the UN Convention against Torture, other Cruel, Inhuman and Degrading Treatment or Punishment.
- Putting into service the international human rights standards against gender-based discrimination[19] as attempted remarkably by Justice K. Ramaswamy in Gaurav Jain[20].

---

19. See The Human Rights Watch Global Report, cited *supra* n. 3 at p. 199.

20. Gaurav Join *v.* Union of India (1997) 8 SCC 114. Understandably many of us will be put off by the description of sex-workers as "fallen women" and by the inaugural invocation, in the first paragraph of the judgment, citing as an epitome of women's achievement such an assortment of "illustrious women leaders" comprising "Indira Gandhi, Margaret Thatcher, Srimovo Bandarnaike"! The texture of the decision is overly paternalistic.

    Despite all this, the interweaving of international human rights instruments and constitutional provisions to sculpt new rights of the girl child from recruitment in sex work industry, is significant. So is the frontal judicial attack into the causes of sex trafficking.

    Kamla is not recalled even now; nor are the labours in Agra Home case, the first full-fledged social action litigation case, presented by Lotika Sarkar and myself (reported fully now in Volume Ill, Supreme Court on Public Interest Litigation, A SCALE/LIPS Publication, New Delhi, 1998 at pp. 966, 1395, 1463, 1663) even referred to!

These are illustrative, not exhaustive,[21] strategies useful only when the movements of human rights find the inclination and time to wrestle the markets in sex-trafficking.

XI

The Manifesto languages stressing the logics and paralogics of solidarity, as against the rather vacuous rhetoric of human rights in the situation of many a Kamla, remains crucial as it traces the passage from the human rights slogan "women's rights are human rights to a right to be and remain a woman."

We know already the litany of interrogations concerning women's rights as human rights. First, it is said to essentialise women as subject positions, which are myriad and diverse. Second, it fixates 'identities' which are heterogeneous and perpetually mobile. Third, all this is to be accomplished in a regime of male-in-the-state. Fourth, this ensures, overall, that women are at the end of the day human rights losers, not winners.[22]

Without depleting the cogency of this important critique, sex trafficking poses the question whether all the enunciations of women's rights as human rights are adequate. If women were truly "integral" with "human" this motto is at best tautologous, at worst misleading. To avoid either extreme, we need to ask, perhaps, what may the transition in the idiom signify.

And the entire vigour of this germinal decision stands now dissipated, at the time of writing, by the important (but wholly irrelevant issue from the standpoint of women's rights as human rights) technical issue of the nature and the scope of judicial power under Article 142 of the Constitution (the power to do "complete justice").

21. For example, the little noted post-CEDAW Inter-American Convention (Convention of Belem do Para). The Convention defines violence "as any act or conduct, based on gender, which causes death or physical, sexual or psychological harm or suffering to women, whether in the public or private sphere." (emphasis added)

22. For all this and more see W. Brown, *supra* n. 9.

The human right to be a woman and to remain so, I believe, addresses the future of human rights.

XII

But what does it signify to say that one is a woman?

Both the contemporaries social and psychoanalytical, as well as many varieties of post-modern discourses problematise the notion of being a "woman."

We know from the classic analysis of kinship by Levi-Strauss that marriage is all about exchange of women "between two groups of men" where the "woman figures only as one of the objects of exchange, not as one of the partners."[23] In this framework, men are exchangers and women "sexual semi-objects."[24] It is true that kinship systems do not "merely exchange women" but create/produce forms of rights that "various people have in other people."[25] But this truth importantly directs our attention to different contextualities, which shape these forms of rights over peoples. It should not necessarily detract from the fact that social life, at its base, as it were, revolves around the "exchange" of women by groups of men in which women signify the order of "sexual semi-objects."

Gayle Rubin has insightfully argued that kinship theorising should go beyond the "acute, but condensed, apprehension of certain aspects of social relations of sex and gender"[26], and especially construct the "political economy of sex." This would include a "full bodied analysis" of "evolution of commodity forms in women, systems of land tenure, political arrangements, subsistence technology" as well

---

23. Claude Levi-Strauss, The Elementary Structures of Kinship, Beacon Press, Boston. 1969, p. 115.
24. Gayle Rubin, "The Traffic in Women: Notes on the Political Economy" of "Sex" in Rayna R. Reiter (ed.), Towards an Anthropology of Women, The Monthly Review Press, New York, 1975. p. 157 at p. 174.
25. *Id.* at p. 177.
26. *Id.* at p. 176.

as marriage and sexuality.[27] But we are still awaiting a feminist version of The Origins of the Family, Private Property and the Slate "recognizing the mutual dependence of sexuality, economics and politics."[28]

Pending such knowledge revolutions, the human right to be a woman may seem to some to be a historically empty enunciation because of pervasive "evolution of commodity forms in women"[29] in which sex trafficking is the norm rather than the exception. Given the obduracy of social formation, the pyhrric 'victory' of social and judicial activism is fully understandable. And so is the sexual destiny of Kamla and her successors in violation. If this is all that the grand tradition of social theory has to offer, the relationship between theoretical production and human rights attainment must remain contradictory.

The enunciation of such a right appears equally vacuous if we were to follow the verities of contemporary psychoanalytical and postmodernist approaches. For example, the post-Freudian French psychoanalyst, Jacques Lacan insists that there is no such thing as a woman. The observation would have some emancipative significance if what was entailed was a denial of thingification or commodity status to women. (Beings are not things. Even so, it is difficult to so acquiesce with Lacan.) But his deeper point, perhaps, is that there is no such being as a woman.

As Drucilla Cornell, following Lacan notes, "to be a woman is always to be differentially" dependent on "race, class, sexuality and age." But she does allow herself to go so far as to say that "there is meaning to the statement that one is a woman even when if that meaning constantly shifts."[30]

What is that constant meaning amidst the many brutal shifts? Put another way, how may an enunciation of a universal human right to be a woman address this multitude of shifting meanings?

---

27. *Id.* at p. 209.
28. *Id.* at p. 210.
29. *Id.* at p. 209 (emphasis added).
30. Drucilla Cornell, "The Philosophy of the Limit: Systems Theory and Feminist Legal Reforms" in D. Cornell *et al.* (eds.), Deconstruction and Possibility of Justice, Routledge, London, 1992, p. 68 at p. 83.

I will have a shorthand[31] recourse to Merlau Ponty who enunciated the notion of justice-in-the-flesh thus:

> [O]ur sense of justice is deeply rooted, firmly grounded in the body of our experience . . . Foucault asks: "what kinds of bodies does our society require?" This is an important question. But it must be coupled with another question: "What kinds of society do our bodies dream?"[32]

The justice-in-the-flesh or the corporeal notion of justice accords a foundational dignity to gender equality in ways no incorporeal notion of justice either aspires or achieves. But what shall we do if "flesh" turns out to be a problematic metaphor?

The articulation of a human right to be, and remain a woman, requires even a further reformulation: "What kind of society do the women's bodies dream?" And, how may the frail vessels of human rights languages convert these dreams, without turning them into nightmares, to performative feats of social transformation?

Will we ever be able to understand the text of women's politics of desire through the narrative of Kamla(s)? And what revision of genres of post-essentialist notions of women may empower struggles on behalf of many a Kamla?

31. Since I have dealt with the problematic in my Mambrino's Helmet: Human Rights for a changing World, Har Anand, New Delhi, 1994, p. 168.
32. Galen A. Johnson and Michael B. Smith (eds.), Ontology and Alterity in Merleau Ponty, Northwestern University Press, Evanston Illinois, 1990, p. 38.

6

Epilogue: Toward Equality

B. SIVARAMAYYA

Owing to initiatives at the international level, the Government of India took an important step towards gender justice in the early seventies namely, to constitute a committee to examine questions relating to rights and status of women in India. Its report is by far the most important document relating to social, legal, political and economic concerns affecting women. A unique feature of this report, unlike other reports, is that it was prepared with the collaboration of specialists drawn from different disciplines who were members of the various task forces.

More than two decades have elapsed since the publication of this pathbreaking Report. It must be noted that an "Empowered Committee" had gone into the recommendations and gave its views on them. The views of the Empowered Committee seem to have guided the thinking of the successive governments at the centre. This article proposes to consider the nature of response of successive governments, their earnestness in carrying out the spirit, if not the letter, of the recommendations of the CSW contained in the Report and the reasons given for not accepting some of the recommendations pertaining to law.

CHILD MARRIAGE

More than sixty years have elapsed since the Child Marriage Restraint Act, 1929 (hereafter CMRA) was passed. But the Act proved to be a dead letter in practice. Child marriages are rampant in many parts of the country especially in the rural areas of Uttar Pradesh, Bihar, Rajasthan and Andhra Pradesh. Media reports in recent years reveal that on the auspicious day of Akshaya Tritiya among the Hindus, thousands of child marriages, even of babies in the arms of their mothers are performed in Rajasthan.

Child Marriage Restraint Act, 1929

It is difficult to exaggerate the effects of such marriages on the parties to the marriage, especially the girls, involving the deprivation of their human rights and destructive of their happiness. It may be recalled that Harbilas Sarda, the moving spirit behind the legislation and after whom the legislation is popularly referred to, observed:

Child marriage is a crime which sometimes results in the death of the victim, the bride and sometimes maiming her for life. . . . The Act primarily deals with a crime, a grave crime against girls. It is an attempt by indirect means to put a stop to the inhuman acts which go unpunished behind the screen of social religious validity. The Child Marriage Restraint Act is a measure which tackles an evil much more grave than sari, because it is far more devastating in its consequences and more insidious in its working.

The CSW report drew attention to the findings of the Committee set-up by the Gujarat Government in 1962, (popularly known as the Pushpaben Committee Report) to investigate the high rate of suicide among young married girls, and pointed out that the Gujarat Committee have child marriage as an important cause for the high rate of suicides.

Of the two recommendations of the CSW report, one pertains to the enforcement measures against child marriages, and the other to what ought to be the policy of law as to the consequences of a child marriage, i.e. whether it should be declared valid or void or voidable

Enforcement

The experience of implementation of the policy against child marriages reveals a casual and half-hearted approach. This is all the more surprising because prevention of child marriages (or marriage of girls who are below the age of 18) is regarded as an important component of the measures against population explosion. Way back in 1974 it was pointed out that "it has been calculated that birth rate in India may be reduced as much as 30% by 1991-92 if all women married after the age of 19." It needs to be pointed out that utter indifference to enforcement plagued the Act both before and after independence.

Enforcement before Independence

Initially the Act had no extra-territorial operation. that is, it did not apply to marriages performed outside the British Indian territories, e.g. the native States and French territories like Yenam and Pondicherry. The result was that many parents solemnised child marriages in these territories where the Act was not in force. Some Native States even derived revenue by imposing a tax on such child marriages. This lacuna in the Act was removed by the Child Marriage Restraint (Second Amendment) Act, 1938.

Again, as Rathbone pointed out, the implementation of the Act was made dependent wholly on private initiative. She stated that the great and corroding evil of child marriage clamours for a remedy but the onus of taking action against it is placed exclusively on a private citizen. The government's spokesman also recognised as much. She rightly questioned "what sort of motive left him to proceed"? She pointed out that it is not pecuniary benefit for himself or pity for the child, he had to incur the wrath of two families and their relations.

If in spite of this a public spirited citizen took steps to set in motion the machinery of the Act, he was made to feel the difficult and thankless nature of the task. To substantiate his bonafides in making the complaint, he had to undergo the humiliation or indignity of executing a security bond.

The Child Marriage Restraint (Second Amendment) Act, 1938 removed the paralysing effects of this provision. The court was empowered to require the complainant to execute a surety in special cases, and when the court required such bond to be executed, it had to record its reasons for doing so. Mercifully, this provision which mocked at public spirited citizens was deleted in 1949.

Obstacles to the Enforcement of the Act

There were many other obstacles in the enforcement of the Act. For example, the offences under the Act were not made cognizable. The reason often given was and is that the police would harass the parties. Granted that police harassment and corruption are true, the question is: would not making the offence cognizable indirectly promote the purpose of the Act, viz. restraining child marriages? It is submitted that police harassment is a lesser evil as compared to the monstrous evil of child marriage.

Another obstacle is the period of limitation fixed for taking cognizance. The existing Section 9 of CMRA says that: No court shall take cognizance of any offence under this Act after the expiry of one year from the date on which the offence is alleged to have been committed.

This provision does not serve to promote the policy and purpose of the Act. Given the weak monitoring system or the absence of it and the influence-peddling that ignores the violations of the Act by the powerful sections of society, it is better that the Damocles sword of prosecution is allowed to hang for a longer duration on the heads of those who solemnised child marriages. Another restraint, even if a minor one, is the immunity of 'omen from the punishment of imprisonment.'

Aspects of Enforcement after Independence

The Gujarat Government in a bid to curb child marriages by an amendment in 1964 made the offences under the Act cognizable offences. It also made a provision for the appointment of Child Marriage Prevention Officers to prevent child marriages and for the effective prosecution of persons solemnizing child marriages. The Pushpaben Committee welcomed these changes.

Experience suggests that for the enforcement of social

reform legislations, it is highly desirable to secure the co-operation of the voluntary agencies. The Gujarat amendment contains a specific enabling Provision in this regard. Section 13(b) of the Gujarat amendment states: "The State Government may associate with each Child Marriage Prevention Officer a non-official advisory body consisting of not more than five social workers, of whom at least two shall be women workers, known within the area of jurisdiction of the officer for the performance of his functions under the Act."

The CSW report after noticing the amendments in Gujarat and Pushpaben Committee's Report, recommended "that all offences under the Child Marriage Restraint Act should be made cognizable and that special officers appointed to enforce the law."

The Empowered Committee's comment on this recommendation was that "this recommendation is not accepted in view of the scope for harassment which such legislation will entail. The Ministry of Law also stated that in Gujarat where it had been tried, results are yet to be noticed."

The question, however, is who is to notice the results of the Gujarat legislation, when and how? Are not three decades since that legislation enough to evaluate the results? Which consideration is more: weighty with the Government of India? The scope for harassment of parents or ruination of the future and happiness of the child? Is this the paradigm of the Government of India's commitment to the rights of the child?

However, in 1978, Parliament amended the CMRA to make the offence cognizable for certain purposes. Section 7 of the CMRA now provides that the Code of Criminal Procedure, 1973 (2 of 1974) shall apply to offences under this Act, as if they are cognizable offences—(a) for purpose of investigation of such offences, and (b) for the purpose of matters other than—(i) matters referred to in Section 42 of that Code; and (ii) the arrest of the person without warrant or without an order of a magistrate.

Making the offence cognizable for certain purposes is a half-hearted approach to a qualitatively grave offence. It also gives an impression to the enforcing authorities that offences under the Act are of lesser gravity.

Child Marriage Restraint Officers

The CSW as pointed out before, recommended the appointment of Child Marriage Prevention Officers. At the operational level, the working of the system reveals some deficiencies which need correction. First, the officers are not provided with transport facilities "to refrain from delay in preventing child marriages." Second, the officers are saddled with other responsibilities unconnected with prevention of child marriages. This should be remedied. Third, there are complaints of political interference when the officers discharge their functions. As such interference will demoralise the officers, it should be avoided at all costs.

Minimum Punishments

The contemporary trend is to provide for minimum punishment for an offence under social legislations. The position under the Protection of Civil Rights Act, 1955 and the Dowry Prohibition Act, 1961 are examples in this regard. Even though the CSW report did not advert to it specifically, for violation of provisions of the CMRA minimum punishments should be prescribed. This would be within the spirit and intendment of the recommendations.

Immunity of Women from Imprisonment

Section 6 of the CMRA deals with punishment to a parent or guardian solemnizing a child marriage. A proviso to clause (d) of the section says "provided that no woman shall be punishable with imprisonment." The report of the CSW is silent on this aspect. But elsewhere Lotika Sarkar advocated for the removal of the restriction, stating that "in one of the cases where the priest had been prosecuted, the judge said that there is a necessity that there must be a deterrent punishment so that people are not encouraged to continue this practice. Some of you might object to it but there is also provision in CMRA which says (that) no woman should be sent for imprisonment. In my opinion this is certainly a case here it is a question of conflict between the interest of the woman and the interest of the child. It would be worthwhile to consider whether the father is the natural guardian or whether there is another legal guardian. But if the former is dead and the mother is the natural guardian and she gets the minor daughter married, why then she should not be punished?

There is thus a strong case for imposing the punishment of imprisonment on a woman, if she as a legal guardian solemnizes a child marriage and for the deletion of proviso to Section 6 sub-section (1) of the CMRA.

Legal Effect of a Child Marriage

Even at the time of passing of the CMRA there were somehow took the view that child marriages should be invalidated. As against this view it was argued that a Hindu marriage was a sacrament and indissoluble, and that if a child marriage is invalidated it would give rise to endless dispute, relating to legitimacy and inheritance of the offspring. As regards the first argument, viz. sacramental nature of Hindu marriage, it should be pointed out that after the enactment of the Hindu Marriage Act, 1955 the sacramental nature of a Hindu marriage is much eroded, if not effaced by divorce, statutory as well as customary, and the increasing to it. The second argument (or its modified form) relating to difficulties in relation to successional rights of children born of such child marriages can be met by making minor modifications and bringing such cases within the ambit of Section 16 of the HMA or such other similar provision to preserve the general applicability of the Act.

Before the CSW three alternatives presented themselves. First was to maintain the *status quo,* that is, to treat the child marriages as valid. Second, to give the victim girl an option to obtain the dissolution of the marriage, whether consummated or not.

It is pertinent to point out that under the Muslim law, when a marriage is consummated the option is unavailable and a progressive interpretation of the rule stated that consummation before she completed the age of fifteen years or before she attained puberty is immaterial. However, the Committee took the view (though unstated) that if the exercise of the right is made contingent on the non-consummation of the marriage, then there would be a trend towards consummation of child marriages as soon the girl attains puberty to avoid the option of puberty and therefore made the right exercisable whether the marriage is consummated or not.

The third alternative is to declare child marriages as void. On this the Committee noted that another effective approach is to render such (child) marriage void. But in the present social and economic conditions, such a rigorous measure may create more problems than it seeks to solve."

Mercifully, the legislature adopted the recommendations of the Committee and enacted Section 13(2)(d) of the Hindu Marriage Act, 1955 (HMA) which conferred an option of puberty to obtain a dissolution of a child marriage, on attaining the age of eighteen, whether the marriage was consummated or not. But this benefit was not extended to other communities like Christians and Parsis, and in the case of Muslims the extension of the remedy to consummated marriages also had been followed.

It should be pointed out that after the adoption of the principle of "option of puberty" under the HMA, in *Suramma* v. *Ganapatuly* (AIR 1975 AP 193) a Division Bench of the Andhra Pradesh High Court held that child marriages, i.e. marriages solemnised in violation of the age requirement specified in Section 5(iii) were void. The court among other things stated: "If we are to agree . . . that by reason of the fact that Sections 11 and 12 do not at all provide for annulment of a marriage solemnised in contravention of cl. (iii) of Section 5 then it will throw open once again the floodgates of child marriages." However, this decision was overruled by the Bench in *P.V. Venkatarama* v. *State* (AIR 1977 AP 43).

It may be argued that very few seem to have taken the benefit of the provision. This is not surprising, as the groups who resort to child marriages are those from poor and uneducated sections of society. Therefore, they are not aware of the evil effects of child marriages or the provisions of the law or the need for complying with them.

The question that requires consideration is whether the time has not arrived to declare child marriage as void. The draft Indian Marriages Bill submitted by the National Commission for Women renders child marriage void. The draft of the Indian Secular Society on Uniform Civil Code also renders marriages void if they violate the condition relating to age of parties. To mitigate the hardship resulting to children born of child marriages, limited legitimacy, as provided under Section 16 of the HMA, may be conferred, enabling them to inherit the properties of their parents.

The suggestion should be implemented only after the creation of a strong enforcement machinery to check child marriages.

Compulsory Registration of Marriages

Even as early as in 1929, the Report of the Age of Consent Committee (hereafter referred to as the Joshi Committee) went into the question of child marriages. It advised certain measures as essential to the success of an enactment to curb child marriages. Amongst them is this that an accurate marriage register in the described form be kept through an administrative department of the government. To facilitate this, it suggested that compulsory notification of marriage must be provided. The Joshi Committee also stated that birth certificates and marriage certificates should be provided free of cost. Referring to compulsory registration of marriages the Census Commission of 1931 stated that "(t)he difficulties of introducing compulsory registration are no doubt great, but it is not easy to see how social legislation can be really effective without it."

Forty-five years later, the Report of the CSW once again emphasised the need for compulsory registration. The Report pointed out that compulsory registration of marriages "operates as an effective check on child and bigamous marriages and also offers reliable proof of marriage."

Recently the National Commission for Women in its draft on the Uniform Law of Marriage and Divorce submitted to the government a proposal emphasising the compulsory registration of marriages. The draft, which is mostly, if not solely, the effort of Justice Chinnppa Reddy, makes registration the proof of marriage, even though the parties may choose to solemnise it in and customary or traditional form.

At the international level, the Convention on the Elimination of Discrimination Against Women in Article 16(2) says that "(t)he betrothal and the marriage of a child shall have no legal effect, and all necessary action, including legislation, shall be taken to specify a minimum age for marriage and to make the registration of marriages in an official registry compulsory." India signed and ratified the convention but with reservations.

Response of Governments

The colonial government's response in not initiating steps to curb child marriages by introducing compulsory registration of marriages was understandable in view of the then context of virulent opposition to the British rule and the then prevailing sentiments in favour of child marriages among the vast majority of Hindus. But Independent India's record in this regard is not only surprising but also condemnable. Only the erstwhile Bombay State (comprising the present-day States of Maharashtra and Gujarat) made marriages compulsorily, registrable under the Bombay Registration of Marriages Act, 1953.

The comment of the Empowered Committee on CSWs recommendation that compulsory registration of marriages should be introduced, may be noted. It said that "(t)he idea is very good and is acceptable. It is already within the rule-making power of the State Governments to make registration of the marriages compulsory. but so far no State Government has yet made it so. In this sphere as in others, education has to go side by side with legislation There are innumerable administrative problems in making registration of marriages compulsory. The decision, therefore, is that in the light of this background, the idea may be tried out in a limited area, may be a Union Territory and the Home Ministry may take the initiative in the matter."

It may be pointed out here that "Entry 5 of the Concurrent List mentions marriage and divorce" and "Entry 30 of the Concurrent List speaks of "vital statistics including registration of birth and deaths." Thus, there is no impediment to the Union Government making registration of marriages compulsory instead of delegating it to the States. If in remote tribal regions the law is difficult to be enforced, it could have specifically excluded such Scheduled Tribes. It needs be pointed out that the changes made in Hindu law by legislations enacted in 1955-56 are not applicable to the Scheduled Tribes unless the Central Government by a notification in the Official Gazette otherwise directs.

Turning to the Convention on Elimination of All Forms of the Discrimination Against Women, the Government of India signed and ratified it with reservations. The reservation relating to compulsory registration says that "though in principle it (Government of Republic of India) fully supports the principle of compulsory registration of marriages, it is no practical in a vast country like India with its variety of customs, religions and level of literacy."

Since 1953 when the erstwhile State of Bombay introduced compulsory registration of marriages, no worthwhile steps were taken to extend compulsory registration of marriages to other States. Instead political inertia, bureaucratic evasion and "passing the buck" have stalled the movement towards compulsory registration of marriages. This manifests the government's insensitivity to the sufferings of women and neglect of its duty to protect children.

JUSTICE FOR WOMEN

It seems natural that a political process obsessed with the garnering of votes should be oblivious to the problems of children. However, the process does not seem to care for the issues affecting women either. We may not notice the nature of considerations that influenced the thinking of the government as reflected in the views of the Empowered Committee on the recommendations of the CSW. The attempt here is not to provide an exhaustive critique of the views of the Empowered Committee on all recommendations of the CSW, but to take as examples some important recommendations of the CSW, the views of the Empowered Committee and the subsequent developments, if any, as regards those aspects.

Mitakshara Coparcenary

The CSW recommended, or to be more accurate, lent its support to the recommendations of the Rao Committee to abolish the right by birth under the Mitakshara law and to convert the Mitakshara coparcenary into a Dayabhaga coparcenary. On this the terse comment of the Empowered Committee was that "(t)his is not acceptable as it is fraught with complications. It is a controversial and much debated issue. It is also to be noted that in another 30-40 years or a generation the matter will only be of academic interest, as the Joint Family is fading out slowly but surely."

The above comment in its reference to "complications" shows a defeatist mentality and even insults the intelligence of the earlier renowned draftsmen of the Hindu Code Bills. Further, almost at the same time when the Empowered Committee gave its view, the Kerala Assembly abolished the right by birth and the joint family system by enacting the Kerala Joint Hindu Family System (Abolition) Act, 1975 without any perceivable legal complications. As regards the pious hope that the discrimination will vanish with the disappearance of joint family, one is entitled to ask what is the purpose of Article 14 which proclaims equality before the law and equal protection of the laws; and Article 15 which prohibits discrimination on the ground of sex?

On the other hand, Andhra Pradesh (1986), Tamil Nadu (1989), Maharashtra (1994) and Karnataka (1994) enacted legislations conferring the right to such property by birth on daughters who were unmarried on the date when the respective legislations came into force. More importantly these four states with one voice and in no uncertain terms declared in the preambles of their respective legislations that the conferment of right by birth on sons only is a violation of Article 14 of the Constitution.

These initiatives of the States, though laudable, indicate that the central government and Parliament can no longer be relied upon in matters concerning legal reform and that qualitatively with respect to women's rights it has abdicated its role. An important fall out of such abdication of responsibility by Parliament will be to foster diversity of approaches in matters concerning law reform and a retreat from the goal of unification of laws. To illustrate, the Mitakshara law after these State legislations in the South stands divided into three types: (1) Mitakshara law as modified by the Hindu Succession Act, 1956, prevailing in the Northern States. (2) Mitakshara law in which statutory the right by birth exists in favour of daughter also; and (3) Mitakshara converted into Dayabhaga by statute as mini Kerala. Thus, the resulting diversity may give rise to more complications than the abolition of Mitakshara coparcenary itself.

Personal laws of Christians in Kerala

On the personal laws of Christians in the former princely States of Travancore and Cochin, the first part of the recommendation stated that "immediate legislative measures are necessary to bring Christian women of Kerala under the Indian Succession Act as a first step to unify the law. It may be recalled that under these personal laws the right of a daughter is restricted to receiving her streedhanam only. In Travancore this was fixed at Rs. 5000 or one-fourth share of a son whichever is less: and in Cochin the daughter's right is restricted to receive streedhanam only if a brother or a lineal descendant of the brother survives the intestate. The latter law did not specify the amount of streedhanam. Under the Succession Act, 1925 a daughter gets the same share as a son. The view of the Empowered Committee on this was that "(t)his is not immediately acceptable. Move for change has to come from the community itself."

Ten years later the Supreme Court in *Mary Roy* v. *State of Kerala* (1986 SCC 209) overruled the decision of the Travancore-Cochin High Court in Kurian

Augusty v. *Devassy A. Ley* held that the Christians in the erstwhile Travancore-Cochin States would be governed by the Succession Act, 1925 after the merger of these States with the Indian Union and not by their personal laws. Regrettably the Supreme Court decided the question on a narrower ground of interpretation of Part B States Laws Act, 1951 and not the wider ground of constitutionality of the discriminatory personal laws. The decision had retrospective effect.

The aftermath of the decision as that furious attempts were made to annul the retrospective operation by means of an ordinance or legislation. It should be noted that for good measure the Church also gave its support to these attempts; but as yet these attempts have not been successful.

The point that needs be noticed is that the decision in Mary Roy, irrespective of or rather in spite of its opposition, served to protect the equal rights of women; whereas government and Parliament failed to do so on narrow political considerations. But to assume that the judiciary can fill the void created by the legislature is to overlook the limitations of the judicial process, viz. it adopts a case by case approach, that it is time-consuming and expensive. It also has to await an opportunity to decide and lay down a new proposition or correct an error of a subordinate court. It cannot obviously remedy in a short time the myriad of discriminator personal laws. Chandrachud, C.J. observed in the Shah Bano case in the context of Article 44: (1985 SCC 556)

We understand the difficulties involved in bringing persons of different faiths and persuasions on a common platform. But a beginning has to be made if the Constitution is to have any meaning. Inevitably, the role of the reformer has to be assumed by the courts because, it is beyond the endurance of sensitive minds to allow injustice to be suffered when it is so palpable. But piecemeal attempts of courts to bridge that gap between personal laws cannot take the place of a Common Civil Code. Justice to all is a far more satisfactory way of dispensing justice than justice from case to case.

The comment of the Empowered Committee gives rise to a basic question: What is the meaning of "community" in the context of minorities? The question is important because the post-independence governments, following or excelling the colonial government, state *ad nausea*, that no reform in the personal laws of Muslims or other minorities would be contemplated without the "community's demand" or without the "community's consent." What is the meaning that should be attached to the word "community" in these phrases? Religious and conservative groups are at odds with reforms, but is that attitude in consonance with the secular character of the Constitution? These expressions can only connote the vocal males who are adversely affected by the reforms.

Women who constitute 50% of these groups should also matter. Were not reforms in Hindu law carried out even in spite of opposition from the majority of men and even women?

Bigamous Marriages among the Hindus

The decision of the Supreme Court in *Bhau Rao* v. *State* (AIR 1965 SC 1564) held that to sustain a conviction for the offence of bigamy the burden lies on the prosecution to establish that the second marriage has been "solemnised" that is, performed with proper ceremonies and in due form. This decision puts a very heavy burden on the prosecution which is often difficult to discharge thereby resulting in few convictions in cases of bigamy. The CSW suggested in its report that the phrase "solemnised" in Section 17 of the Hindu Marriage Act, 1955 should be replaced by the words goes through a form of marriage and that an explanation should be added to the section to the effect that an omission to perform some of the essential ceremonies by the parties should not be construed to mean that the offence of bigamy was not committed, if such a ceremony gave rise to a *de facto* relationship of husband and wife.

Referring to this the Empowered Committee observed: 'The objective in the recommendation would be achieved by an amendment to Sections 494 and 495 of the IPC proposed by the Joint Select Committee in the Bill now before Parliament." But nothing came out of the Bill regarding amendments to Sections 494 and 495 of the IPC. Nor did the amendments to HMA in 1976 and 1978 incorporate the recommendations of the CSW. Thus the recommendation was made to fall between the two stools of IPC and HMA.

Polygamy under Muslim Law

The report of the CSW stated that they were of the firm view that there could be no compromise on the basic policy of monogamy being the rule for all communities in India. Adverting specifically to the reform to correct the abuse of polygamy, the CSW noted that "(w)hile the desirability of reform in Muslim law is generally acknowledged . . . the government has taken no step towards changing the law for over two decades on the view that public opinion in the Muslim community did not favour a change. But this view cannot be reconciled with the declaration of equality and social justice. We are, therefore, of the opinion that ignoring the interest of Muslim women is denial of social justice. The right to equality, in our view, like the right to free speech, is an individual right."

The Empowered Committee responded that "the recommendation is accepted in principle. However, it would be expedient to generate proper attitudinal changes among the members of the Muslim community before introducing legislation. . . ."

It will be of interest to know that on the question of reform of Muslim law to correct the abuse of polygamy. Some members of the Empowered Committee felt about this Mantra, "(w)ait for the minority community to get education, move for reform and then propose changes", that it would mean "we would have to wait for eternity and that government would do well to take some steps to force the change." Needless to add that the government would prefer "to wait for eternity" rather than force changes in Muslim law.

Triple Talak

Muslim law confers on the husband a unilateral power to divorce and the exercise of this power has been a matter of considerable concern to all interested in the status of Muslim women. Adverting to this aspect, the report of the CSW says: "But the power of the husband to pronounce talak unilaterally remains, and has in no way been curtailed either judicially or through legislation. As long as this absolute and unlimited right remains, the position of the Muslim wife will remain secure and her status cannot be raised."

Without specifically referring to each of the recommendations on divorce, and clubbing the recommendations on Muslim and Christian laws, the Empowered Committee dismisses them with a laconic statement. Here again the move for reform will have to come from the minority communities themselves. Therefore, these recommendations are not accepted."

recommendations are not accepted."

Among the unilateral forms of divorce, the commonly used mode of divorce by the Hanafis is the triple talak, that is, saying thrice "I divorce thee" or "I divorce thee thrice." Such divorce when once pronounced becomes irrevocable and is an unapproved form of divorce. Recently a Single Judge of the Allahabad High Court in *Rahamat Ullah* v. *State of U.P.* and *Khatoon Nisa* v. *State of U.P.* held that triple talak (talak-ul-bidai) is invalid and cannot be recognised as a valid divorce. The decision attracted much media attention and an appeal is pending before the Supreme Court against the decision.

Restrictions on Testations

Most legal systems have restrictions on testamentary power. It is only the Common Law that follows the principle of unrestricted power to dispose of property by means of a will. A learned editor of Jarman writing in 1951 observed: "Complete freedom of testation, as enjoyed under English law for a brief period of forty-seven years, is therefore by the standards of comparative jurisprudence an anomaly." Roman law, Muslim law and Civil law systems prevailing in Europe, South America and in some states in the USA have restrictions on testation.

The CSW in its report said that "(t)he Committee's own experience in many places, but particularly in Banaras more than proves the point that there are mens' women who have been reduced to destitution and beggary because their families have deprived them of all support." Further, it said: "We recommend that the right of testation should be limited under the Hindu Succession Act, so as not to deprive legal heir completely." Earlier the same recommendation as made with respect to the Succession Act, 1925, while dealing with succession to Christians

The comment of the Empowered Committee was that (t)his is not acceptable. For one thing restricting this right may lead to unwise distribution of property during lifetime. For another, this law does not affect large majority of people.

The first reason given by the Empowered Committee mocks at the rich experience of the other legal systems in

India and abroad. Do restrictions on testation under Muslim law lead to an unwise distribution of property during one's lifetime? These legal systems bring within the definition of testamentary disposition certain transfers *inter vivos* like gifts or transfers with nominal considerations to check the evasion of restrictions on testation.

Nearer home, Muslim law considers marz-ul-maut gifts as being within the limitation imposed on testamentary disposition. The laws of Goa, Daman and Diu, based on Portuguese Civil Code impose testamentary restrictions. Article 1784 dealing with legitime or compulsory portion lays down: "Legitime means the portion of the properties the testator cannot dispose of, because it has been set apart by law for the lineal descendants or ascendants.

Sole Paragraph: This portion consists of half of properties of the testator. . . ."

Article 1457 subjects gifts *mortis causa* to the rules and restrictions applicable to wills and Article 1495 lays down the order of reduction in respect of gifts when they adversely affect legitime.

The second cryptic comment of the Empowered Committee that "this law does not affect large majority of people" is enigmatic. Unrestricted testamentary power over their properties can be exercised by all communities barring Muslims. In the case of male Hindus, not only their separate and self-acquired properties but even their share in the joint family property could be the subject-matter of testamentary disposition. If it is meant that a vast majority of people are illiterate and do not make wills, the statement is questionable as even illiterate people can execute wills by putting their thumb impression. At any rate there are indications that wills are now executed primarily to disinherit daughters. This aspect has not been noticed by the Empowered Committee.

UNIFORM CIVIL CODE

An important recommendation of the CSW pertains to the Directive Principle contained in Article 44, viz. that the State should endeavour to secure for its citizens a Uniform Civil Code. The CSW in its report recommended its expeditious implementation; whereas the Empowered Committee gave it sanjeevini, the cure all, stating that "(t)he question is one of proper timing to undertake amendments of the various laws so as to achieve uniformity. It is hoped that with the continuous education through mass media and other communication channels, a climate is paved for effecting reform. The recommendation of the Empowered Committee is that we should work towards achieving this result before the end of the Decade for Women."

At the end of the Decade for Women the reverse happened. The obiter in Shah Bano on Uniform Civil Code caused tremors in the Muslim community leading to the enactment of the Muslim Women's (Protection of Rights on Divorce) Act, 1986.

Even as regards the Uniform Civil Code, the Supreme Court urged for its enactment as an "objective observer" that is to say, motivated by a desire to alleviate the hardships and sufferings of women. As noted earlier, referring to Article 44 Chandrachud, CJ noted that "(t)here is no evidence of any official activity for framing a common civil code for the country. A belief seems to have gained ground that it is for the Muslim community to take a lead in the matter of reforms of their personal law. . . . No community is likely to bell the cat by making gratuitous concessions on this issue. It is the state which is charged with the duty of securing a Uniform Civil Code."

Shortly after Shah Bano, Justice Chinnappa Reddy in *Jorden Diengdeh* v. *S.S. Chopra* (1985 Sec. 62) had occasion to point out the official dithering on Uniform Civil Code. There, a woman belonging to the Khasi tribe, a Christian, married S.S. Chopra under the Christian Marriage Act, 1872 and later sought a decree of nullity under the Divorce Act, 1869, which is more than a century old. The Supreme Court noted that "(t)he case before us is an illustration of a case where the parties are bound together by a marital tie which is better untied." Justice Chinnappa Reddy pointed out the archaic nature of the provision of the Divorce Act applicable to Christians as compared to the Hindu Marriage Act, 1955, and the diverse nature of matrimonial remedies applicable to different religious denominations. He observed that "(t)he totally unsatisfactory state of affairs on the lack of a Uniform Civil Code is exposed by the facts of the present case."

Once again, the Supreme Court in *Sarla Mudgal* v. *Union of India* (1995 SCC 635) emphasised the need for a Uniform Civil Code. There an organisation called Kalyani through its president brought before the Supreme Court four cases which involved fake conversion to Islam by Hindu husbands to contract bigamous marriages. It sought the decision of the Supreme Court on the questions: (i) Whether a Hindu husband married under the Hindu law, by embracing Islam can solemnise a second marriage? (ii) Whether such a marriage without having the first marriage dissolved under law would be a valid marriage qua the first wife who continues to be a Hindu? (iii) Whether the apostate husband would be guilt) of the offence under Section 494 .of the Indian Penal Code?

Kuldip Singh (Sahai, J. concurring) answered the question thus: "We hold that the second marriage of a Hindu husband after conversion to Islam, without having the first marriage dissolved under law, would be invalid. The second marriage would be void in terms of the provisions of Section 494 IPC and the apostate-husband would be guilty of the offence under Section 494 IPC."

Kuldip Singh J. in his judgment referred to the observations of Chandrachud, C.J. in Shah Bano and of Chinnappa Reddy, J. in Jorden Diengdeh's case urging the Union Government to evolve the Uniform Civil Code. He then proceeded to say that "One wonders how long will it take for the Government of the day to implement the mandate of the framers of the Constitution under Article 44 of the Constitution of India. There is no justification whatsoever in delaying indefinitely the introduction of a uniform personal law in the country."

In my view the best observation on the subject has been made by Sahai, J. in his concurrent opinion. He stated: "But religious practices, violative of human rights and dignity and sacerdotal suffocation of essentially civil and material freedoms, are not autonomy but oppression. Therefore, a unified code is imperative both for the protection of the oppressed and promotion of national unity and solidarity. But the first step should be to rationalise the personal law of minorities to develop religious and cultural amity."

THE NEW PATRIARCHY

Almost coinciding with the report of the CSW a new patriarchy has emerged on the Indian scene, more subtle in its form and more sophisticated in its appearances than the crude patriarchy of by gone times. It wears different masks in tune with times like social justice, minority rights, pluralism, cultural rights. In the seventies it took the name of social justice and subordinated the rights of women. For example, under the land ceiling legislations of various States while an additional unit of ceiling or land was given in the case of an adult son, no such additional land was given in the case of the daughter. Most of the land legislations were included in the Ninth Schedule and thereby gained immunity from constitutional challenge. Nonetheless, the Supreme Court considered the validity of this provision in *Ambika Prasad Mishra* v. *State of U.P.* (1980 SCC 719) Krishna Iyer, J., delivering the judgment of the court upheld the provision stating, "(t)hat provision shows a concession to a tenure-holder who has propertyless adult sons by allowing him to keep two more hectares per such son. The propertyless son gets no right to a cent of land on this score but the father is allowed to keep some more of his own for feeding this extra mouth." Referring to the above it can said, "Presumably adult daughters need not to be fed."

As regards reforms in Hindu law in 1955-56 Baxi says: (i) Upendra Baxi, "Muslim Law Reform, Uniform Civil Code and die Crisis of Common Sense", in Tahir Mahmood (ed.). Family Law and Social Change, Indian Law Institute, New Delhi, 1975, p. 21. "It is true that Hindu personal law was rationalised by coercive legal means." By the same token, the regulation prohibiting sati, the Hindu Widows Remarriage Act, 1856 and Child Marriage Restraint Act, 1929 are coercive legislations because there were more opponents to these measures than the supporters. By the same standard, abolition of slavery in the USA and of untouchability in India should be regarded as coercive. The point is that the granting of legal equality even partly, in case of Hindu women, and more so in the case of Muslim women is regarded as resort to coercion, and not as enforcement of their entitlements. This, as noticed before, is perfectly in accord with the attitude of the government which believes that certain groups can veto the equal legal status of women. Baxi further says that the modernist must do his "homework", i.e., have draft for discussion. Whatever may be the position when he wrote the article, as of now on marriage and divorce four drafts are available, (1) one submitted by the National Commission for Women, (2) one prepared by the Indian Secular Society, Pune, (3) Law Ministry's draft buried under the files as confidential, (4) the draft of the Bar Council of India. As regards adoption. the recent legislation passed by the State of Maharashtra, that is, the Maharashtra Adoption Act, 1995, will serve as a good model and a similar exercise can be undertaken with regard to succession: otherwise the provisions of the Succession Act, 1925 can form the basis of the law.

Yet another laboured point of Baxi's article is that the modernist should have a dialogue with the ulema and try to convince them. Suffice it to say that this is an exercise in futility.

Vasudha Dhagamwar, from Indian Law Institute, Delhi, Baxi's concern that "Uniform Civil Code should not be used to foist Hindu law on the nation." It must be remembered that the Hindu Marriage Act, 1956 has drawn largely from the then English law on matters concerning matrimonial reliefs and that the Hindu Succession Act, 1955, borrowed the principle of simultaneous succession from Muslim law. In any event the existing drafts could be scrutinised to allay such fears.

Great jurist Shri Tarkunde is of the view that "the change (in personal law) has to be supported by substantial part of the educated and liberal sections of the community."

The journey towards equality of women is thus long and arduous. We despair seeing the journey's end in our lifetimes but nonetheless hope that the wait will not be long after; and certainly not for eternity.

Index